COACHING

WITH IMP

C000071127

COACHING
WITH IMPACT AT WORK

GILL GRAVES

RƎTHINK PRESS

First Published in Great Britain 2015
by Rethink Press (*www.rethinkpress.com*)

© Copyright Gill Graves

For Colin – the brightest and the best

For where we'll be and where we've been
Is always where we are.
And everything that comes your way
Is something you once gave.
Somebody feels the water
Every time you make a wave.

THOM BISHOP

PRAISE

'Gill possesses great insights into getting the best out of leaders and managers. She gets to the heart of people's personality and motivation and makes a real difference to their self-awareness and performance. I have worked with Gill many times in Cambridge and I have always seen her bring huge benefits to executives and the way they think and behave. Her background, knowledge and action focus make her a very inspiring individual'

Philip Stiles, Co-Director of the Centre for International Human Resource Management (CIHRM) Judge Business School University of Cambridge

Gill has equipped our coaches with the skills and confidence to enter the coaching world of work – to provide professional, credible, coaching excellence. Gill's creativity and challenge really helps to unlock people's thinking so that they can achieve so much more!

Nadia Harrington, Founder of the Suffolk Coaching and Mentoring Partnership

Gill Graves is an exceptionally gifted coach. She combines an attention to detail with a desire to work with and help those she is coaching and has the emotional intelligence and skills to bring about meaningful change. She stretches and questions while also supporting you. As a result Gill succeeds in getting her clients to see and approach situations in a different way.

Jeremy Roche, Dean and Director of Studies, Faculty of Health and Social Care, The Open University

Working with Gill as my coach has been both an invaluable and enjoyable experience. She has helped me find simple and effective tools that improve performance and boost my self-confidence. Our sessions are very effective as my trust in Gill is such that I can share anything with her. Everyone should have a Gill in their life.

Catherine Gormley, General Manager, Faccenda Foods

Gill did a great job for our multinational client in Shanghai in building a coaching culture through coaching workshops for managers and team leaders around the company. She is very open, passionate and experienced. She adapted her teaching style naturally and participants benefited a lot from her workshop which is practical designed. I look forward to having Gill in China for more days in the coming year!
Renee Yu Yixia, Cambridge Pragmatix China

Gill developed a good rapport with me very quickly and over the course of our sessions it was clear that she not only knew her subject extremely well but also had extensive knowledge of working in senior roles herself. My sessions with Gill have given me the confidence that there isn't any challenge that I can't face in my professional or personal life and I am already missing her encouraging smiles!
Donna McGrath FCCA, Chief Finance Officer, Shropshire Clinical Commissioning Group

Gill coaches individuals in an engaging and non-threatening way to explore their world below the iceberg tip of technical skills and competencies. She gently, yet effectively, draws out what behaviours and activities can energize a person, both present and future, that can optimize their personal and professional impact.
Neil Walker, Chief Contract and Performance Officer, Solihull Clinical Commissioning Group

One of the best courses I've ever been on and has left a lasting impression. Really hit the spot with me and has led me to launch a coaching culture in my organization. Gill is superb on every count – knowledge, style, warmth, humour and professionalism.
Sally Peckham, Recruitment and Development Business Partner, Ipswich Borough Council

FOREWORD

I am delighted that Gill Graves has decided to put pen to paper once more. Not only has she a wonderfully accessible, clear style, but Gill offers her readers the richness of her long experience in business and in coaching. Gill is an accredited EMCC master practitioner, has a Masters in coaching and mentoring from Oxford Brooks and a Diploma in Coaching Supervision from the Coaching Supervision Academy. In addition, she has an MBA from Warwick and a vast array of tools and trainings, which have equipped her to be the excellent practitioner that she is. This depth of commitment and experience means that these chapters contain plenty that will stimulate both the experienced coach and those who are new to the profession.

The gift of her long experience for the reader is that Gill brings to current coaching literature a wide knowledge of coaching methodologies, coaching contexts and key coaching topics. The chapters in this book amply illustrate her capacity to speak intelligently across the full range of coaching themes. She generously shares her insights with the reader – insights which have been garnered from many years of experience and training. This book is practical and accessible and it educates the reader in many of the contemporary coaching discourses: coaching relationships, change theory, leadership, self-management, reflection and resilience. As Gill takes the reader through this territory, it is so obvious that she has been around the block and the reader benefits from her thorough knowledge combined with her hands-on understanding of the situations that coaches face every day.

Coaches will love having such clear, informed and detailed discourse on key elements of their everyday working experience. This is a book that will bear re-reading; it is also a book to dip into again and again. I imagine that it will become a valued companion to many coaches.

Edna Murdoch
Director, Coaching Supervision Academy

PREFACE

I first met Gill when she engaged me as her supervisor during her training as a coaching supervisor with the Coaching Supervision Academy. From the very start and what has remained constant is Gill's down-to-earth approach both personally and professionally. While she has a very strong theoretical underpinning in her coaching, supervision and training practice, she always looks to explore issues and find solutions that are clear and practical, using 'layperson's' terms wherever possible, uncluttered with jargon. I know with Gill that she is always willing to try out new approaches and experiment with fresh ideas. She is imaginative and creative in how she tackles issues, be this for one to one or group interventions and activities. She works easily with a wide variety of creative tools from drawing to picture cards to post-its or natural objects which enables her to find fresh insights and awareness for herself and her clients. Using these tools has frequently enabled us to look beyond the immediate presenting situations and see how these fit into the wider systems within which she works.

Gill brings all of herself to our work and I imagine that she is the same with her clients. I really appreciate her honesty and authenticity which inspires and touches me and which is probably the same for anyone she works with. While she takes her professionalism seriously, she has a wonderful capacity to laugh and take herself lightly and at the same time shows real compassion for the foibles of being human.

I'm confident that Gill's practical, powerful exercises and interventions here will expand your capacity to facilitate learning and change with your clients. If you can apply these with some of Gill's light touch and bring some of her fun into your own approach, you and your clients will be laughing with delight and learning a lot.

Dr Alison Hodge
Executive Coach and Coaching Supervisor

INTRODUCTION

So you've picked up a copy of *Coaching with Impact* at a bookshop, downloaded it online; or maybe someone has purchased a copy of it for you, or you're wondering whether to buy a copy yourself... You may be asking yourself, 'Do I need another book on coaching? How will this book help me? Is it worth me investing my valuable time to read it? What makes *Coaching with Impact* different and special?'

In my work as a coach, coach supervisor and trainer of coaches I hear a lot of frustration from people in the initial stages of learning how to coach that, whilst there are a lot of books about what coaching is and 'best practice', there are very few focussing on how to coach that include practical tools and techniques for developing coaches to try out.

For several years I've run Institute of Leadership and Management (ILM) level 5 and level 7 coaching programmes. When I ask delegates for feedback on the programme they've just completed I'm consistently told that they loved how practical it was, the breadth of tools and techniques they had been introduced to and the fact that some of these were very practical whilst others were quite different and creative. Over the years I've noticed that many trainee coaches have started to develop their own coaching tool kit by the end of a programme and they proudly share with me the contents of their own 'magic box', collection of postcards, buttons, photographs, etc. Better still, many of these coaches have gone on to establish their own coaching practices and I'm now the frequent recipient of new materials to add to my own tool kit.

Of course being a highly effective coach is not just about using lots of tools and techniques. I always say to my trainee coaches that fundamentally I believe we need to be really good at three things to be a great coach.

1. The ability to make a genuine connection with your coachees.
2. Listening skills. By this I mean really listening; listening with our whole bodies rather than just simply hearing what somebody says. I would also add that in this context listening also includes the ability to hold a silence – without being compelled to fill it with our own words.
3. The ability to ask really effective coaching questions. Questions which challenge people to think differently and to start coming up with solutions for themselves.

If we are doing the above skilfully then we can be highly effective coaches. Sometimes the simple approach is the best approach. I also believe that we can enhance our coaching practice by having a wider and deeper understanding of different techniques and perspectives, and that having recourse to an alternative way of looking at an issue or idea can help our coachees unlock something and start to think about a way forward. *Coaching with Impact* is therefore intended as a one-stop tool kit for developing coaches, or anyone who is looking to adopt a more coaching approach in their work. The book covers the coaching fundamentals outlined above of: making a connection, listening and asking questions. It then proceeds to introduce a wide array of practical and creative tools and techniques, many of which I have developed in my own coaching work and all of which I use in my own coaching practice. Throughout the book there are step-by-step instructions for activities, enabling you to try these out immediately in your own work.

In the words of Edna Murdoch of the Coaching Supervision Academy, 'Who we are is how we coach™' – and I truly believe this. Who we are as a person, our values, beliefs and sense of identity, infuses all that we do and affects how we coach others and develop our own unique style. Which brings me to my own coaching style and, therefore, the essence of this, my coaching book.

I'm often asked to describe my coaching methodology. Do I favour any particular models and techniques? Do I follow a specific framework or approach? My well-rehearsed response is that my approach is 'eclectic'.

I'm conscious that my coaching style is shaped by a variety of sources. I come from a creative and musical family. My father was a music teacher and my mother a trained singer so I grew up surrounded by the arts and was encouraged to make music, read, enjoy arts and crafts and visit the theatre. My older sister followed in my father's footsteps and became a music teacher, whilst I took a different, but related, route and read English Literature at university.

This early period of creativity began to be submerged when I started work. I chose human resources as a career – probably a career associated more with processes and procedures than creativity! Nevertheless it was a career I thoroughly enjoyed, and I was fortunate to spend many years at a company I loved and with fantastic, bright people.

Looking back I find it hard to remember precisely when I started coaching. Twenty plus years ago, whilst in my former job, I remember attending a series of coaching skills workshops where we were introduced to the GROW Model and did some interesting outdoor activities simulating skiing using planks and pieces of rope. I recall carrying out a few mini coaching sessions with my team, practising asking my coaching questions and active listening.

When I set up my own business in 2000, I qualified to use a number of psychometrics including the Myers Briggs Type Indicator (MBTI) and the Occupational Personality Questionnaire (OPQ32). My coaching started to take the format of a feedback session exploring the individual's profile, followed by some 'coaching' around next steps and what they were going to do with their newfound knowledge. I recall some of the tension I experienced from having to learn to use a tool correctly alongside my natural inclination to ask whatever question came to mind.

A couple of years later I discovered Neuro Linguistic Programme (NLP) and became fascinated by the rich array of tools and techniques sitting under the umbrella of NLP. I completed an introduction to NLP, quickly followed by my Business Practitioner, Master Practitioner and finally a Train the Trainer course. By now I was doing quite a lot of coaching and was starting to call myself a coach. Looking back, my coaching sessions were still quite structured. I would often arrive at a coaching session knowing that we would be exploring neurological levels of change or perceptual positions or another tool that day. I was still following a process, albeit with more tools and techniques available to use.

In the mid-2000s I decided the time had come to get formally qualified as a coach and I enrolled on an

Advanced Diploma in coaching. I immediately became reacquainted with the GROW Model and started to use this in my coaching sessions. Soon I discovered that the GROW Model could be 'improved' upon by including some of the well-formed outcome questions from NLP and I started to develop my own style of coaching. I continued studying and completed an MA in Coaching and Mentoring. The course introduced me to some new perspectives, in particular psychotherapeutic approaches – transactional analysis, Gestalt and person-centred therapy. My curiosity was now fully awakened and I found myself attending more and more courses to learn about different approaches and integrating these techniques into my coaching practice.

My style was becoming increasingly eclectic. The days of slavishly following the GROW Model had gone. Whilst GROW had served me well for coaching individuals who had performance-related or skill-based tasks, I was finding it less useful for transformational change, for example coaching a newly-promoted Finance Director who was wanting to develop their self-awareness and understand their impact on others. My coaching style was evolving and I was beginning to follow my intuition rather than follow any particular model. I was also starting to rediscover the creative me and introduce some slightly 'different' activities into my coaching.

In 2010 I decided to train to be a Coach Supervisor. Having researched a number of providers, I decided to train with the Coaching Supervision Academy (CSA) which specialises in creative and psychotherapeutic approaches to coaching and supervision. I started to work with a coaching supervisor, Alison Hodge, and went on to join a creative supervision group, again run by Alison.

Although the approaches we used were being used in the context of coach supervision, I found most were equally applicable to coaching and started to introduce them into my coaching practice. By now my style was truly eclectic.

I have continued to run my coaching practice and my accredited coaching skills training programmes in this way. I'm a great believer in first getting the basics right and then continuing to develop your practice so that you can integrate new tools, techniques and approaches into your coaching work.

Five years' ago I published my first book, *Presenting Yourself with Impact at Work*. I hadn't particularly intended the book to be a coaching book and was quite surprised when I received comments from practising coaches that they had really enjoyed the book, used a number of the activities with their coaching clients and that, on their recommendation, a number of their clients had read the book. 'So when are you writing your coaching book?' became a familiar question.

As we will explore in Chapter Four, questions are a fundamental part of coaching. Once we've been asked a question we're programmed to answer it, and our unconscious mind will continue to work on any unanswered questions. So my unconscious mind was starting to think about my next book. Eventually I decided to write a coaching manual that would reflect my own coaching style – an eclectic 'tapas' of tools and techniques that coaches could select and try out in their own coaching practice. The first seeds of *Coaching with Impact* were sown...

The word 'Impact' is important to me and chosen quite deliberately. The dictionary definition of impact is 'a powerful effect that something, especially something new, has on a situation or person', which is literally what I believe effective coaching is. It isn't about having cosy chats and sympathising with people. Used effectively, coaching is an incredibly powerful tool for enabling people to bring about their own change.

Coaching with Impact is intended as a resource to be read as a whole, or alternatively dipped into if you are coaching someone with a particular issue/on a specific subject and would like some different insights.

SUMMARY OF THE CHAPTERS:

The chapters are organised so that the fundamentals of coaching are covered first.

What is coaching? This first chapter explores some of the different approaches to coaching, the spectrum of coaching and the characteristics of an effective coach.

Getting ready to coach. This chapter focuses on some of the key considerations before we embark on coaching, as either the coachee or the coach. The chapter includes some useful questions to ask coachees to prepare them for coaching as well as covering the importance of 'contracting' on both an informal and more formalised basis.

Creating the coaching space. This chapter explores the importance of creating a coaching space and offers some insights into how to do so, including building rapport and levels of listening.

Questions, questions, questions! This chapter covers one of the most useful tools for coaching – asking questions. I have included a variety of forms of questions – from challenging, powerful questions to more non-directive 'clean' questions.

Goals, issues, ideas? In order to coach someone, they need to have something to work on. In coaching this is often referred to as a goal. My own experience of coaching is that invariably people turn up for coaching without a nice neat goal. Instead they may have an idea, an overall concept of what they want. Equally they may be seeking to work with a coach because they have an issue, a bit of a knotty problem that they want to explore. Either way, as a coach we need to work with our coachee to give them clarity on what it is they want to focus on in coaching.

The GROW Model. Chapter Six provides a detailed exploration of the GROW model, including an explanation of each stage and some useful questions to ask. This chapter is intended for those relatively new to coaching who would find a framework and sample questions a useful starting point.

Chapters Seven to Fourteen are what I call 'play' chapters. I have quite deliberately used the word 'play' as it is a word I often use in coaching. 'Shall we just have a play with x…?' is a phrase I use a lot. 'Play' has a number of connotations for me. Firstly it speaks of being a light touch. When we play with a tool or technique we use it lightly, to shine a light on an issue, to give a different perspective. It's not about slavishly using the tool, focussing on being correct or going through something from start to finish. By inviting someone to play, I'm inviting them to do something which is: enjoyable; has relaxed rules; can start, stop or be paused as required. Each of the chapters is centred on a different theme for coaching.

Chapter Seven is a 'tapas' of tools and techniques for exploring work-life balance and career transitions.

Chapter Eight focuses on tools and techniques for understanding responses to change and managing change.

Chapter Nine looks at tools and techniques for building resilience.

Chapter Ten adopts a creative approach to exploring 'tricky' relationships.

Chapter Eleven provides a transactional analysis framework for exploring 'tricky' relationships.

Chapter Twelve focuses on frameworks and tools for coaching from a strengths-based perspective.

Chapter Thirteen provides a structure for working with self-management and self-control.

Chapter Fourteen focuses on leadership styles and Authentic Leadership.

Developing reflective practice. I have deliberately ended the book with a chapter on reflection. So many coaching models end at action. However, as coaches I believe one of the most valuable skills we can pass on to our coachees is taking time to reflect: to extract the learning from something and think about how we could do something differently next time. This chapter also includes our own time to reflect as a coach, including the vital discipline of supervision.

Come to the edge.
We might fall.
Come to the edge.
It's too high!

COME TO THE EDGE!

And they came,
and he pushed,
and they flew.

Christopher Logue

CHAPTER ONE

WHAT IS COACHING?

You've no doubt chosen this book because you have an interest in coaching. Maybe you are already a practising coach looking for some new ideas. Maybe you are a manager seeking to use more of a coaching style with your team. Alternatively you have been coached and are now looking to explore the principles and fundamentals of coaching. Or perhaps you just have a general interest in coaching. Whatever your reason for reading, the word 'coaching' will already mean something to you. So let's start by exploring some of the definitions of coaching.

Definitions of coaching tend to group around two different schools of thought: learning and development linked to performance improvement, or coaching to facilitate personal growth and change. Speaking from the learning and development standpoint, Downey (1999, p.21) defines coaching as 'The art of facilitating the performance, learning and development of others'. Parsloe and Wray (2000, p.42) agree, emphasising the importance of learning and development in the process of performance improvement: 'A process that enables learning and development to occur and thus performance to improve'. More recently, Rogers (2004, p.7) offers her own definition, again referring to the important role of learning: 'The coach works with clients to achieve speedy, increased and sustainable effectiveness in their lives and careers through focussed learning'. The last definition is of particular interest in that it not only emphasises the role of learning, but how this form of learning is sustainable.

By contrast, others have argued that coaching is much more about change than learning and development; often transformational change.

People come to coaching for lots of different reasons, but the bottom line is change. They no longer want things to stay the same and they see that coaching can make that happen. (Whitmore, 2002, p.27).

Flaherty (1999, p.3-4) appears to agree, identifying three products of coaching: 'Long-term excellent performance'; 'self-correction'; and 'self-generation', all of which emphasise the change and sustainability aspects of coaching. Hawkins and Smith (2006) take the theme of change even further, referring to their coaching approach as 'systemic transformational coaching', which, they argue, is different to coaching approaches 'that focus on either skill or awareness or insight as the primary goals for progress' (p.28).

The above definitions raise an interesting question as to how much the coach's own perspective of coaching determines their approach as a coach, including the tools and techniques they use. Personally, I like Bluckert's (2005) broad-based definition of coaching, encompassing both learning and change:

Coaching is the facilitation of learning and development with the purpose of improving performance and enhancing effective action, goal achievement and personal satisfaction. It invariably involves growth and change, whether that is in perspective, attitude or behaviour (p.173).

There are, therefore, many different definitions of the term 'coaching'. Some consistent themes emerging from these definitions include:

Coaching is the art of facilitating another person's learning, development and performance. Through coaching, a person is able to find their own solutions, develop their own skills and change their own behaviours and attitudes.

Coaching is an on-going process designed to help others gain greater competence and overcome barriers to improving performance.

Coaching enables others to achieve goals by using their own inner resources.

THE SPECTRUM OF COACHING SKILLS

At the heart of coaching is a relationship, and the conversation that takes place within that relationship can take a number of forms depending on the situation and the

Figure 1 The Spectrum of Coaching Skills

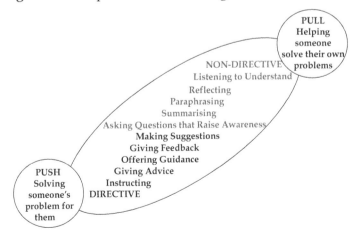

needs. Figure 1 displays most of the different conversational approaches a coach might take during a coaching session.

The most important distinction made in the diagram is between directive and non-directive coaching. Directive means just that: to direct, to tell, to instruct. It is the form of education and management that we are most familiar with. It has its genesis in our earliest days and then all the way through our schooling.

Directive coaching has some distinct advantages and there will be occasions when it is the appropriate approach to take: for example, teaching new skills when the coach has particular expertise to share and when time is precious.

Several years ago I was facilitating on a leadership programme. On the fourth afternoon we were taken down to the local rowing club, split into two groups of eight and given twenty minutes of rowing coaching. We were told exactly what to do, how to do it, what not to do and given instant feedback on anything that we did incorrectly. After twenty minutes we were divided into two rowing boats and took part in a short race. Looking back this was the most directive form of coaching I think I've ever experienced! But of course it had to be. We only had twenty minutes, none of us could row and, as you'll know if you've ever rowed in an eight, you can't just stop rowing – you have to carry on and work with the rest of the crew.

Somewhere in the middle of this continuum is what I refer to as 'mixed coaching'. Here an individual may be seeking to improve their general performance, for example the impact of personal style. As before, the coach may have expertise to share, but the way in which this is shared is slightly different. Here the emphasis will be on providing some information, followed by the opportunity for the individual to have a go, obtain some feedback and take part in facilitated reflection.

For many years one of my specialisms has been presence and impact work, and this was the subject of my first book, *Presenting Yourself with Impact*. When working in this space, either running workshops or on a one-to-one basis, 'mixed coaching' is my preferred modus operandi. I tend to impart a few hints and tips or good practice, give the individual an opportunity to have a go and then facilitate a time for reflection, always starting with what the individual thought they did well or could have done better before providing any feedback of my own. Mixed coaching includes the personal opinion, view, etc. of the coachee much more than directive coaching. However, at least in the short-term, it takes longer.

At the far right end of the spectrum is non-directive coaching. Again the title says it all – you do not direct, instruct or tell. Think about how you learned to crawl and then finally walk. You learned through direct experience, through trial and error. Unconsciously, your body-mind processed the information gained from that experience, took account of the results, and made the appropriate corrections. Each one of us is born with an innate capacity to learn. A non-directive coach seeks to tap into that instinct so that the person learns for themselves.

Non-directive coaching is particularly suited for long-term development/personal issues (e.g. career planning, work-life balance concerns) and encourages the coachee to learn by facilitated reflection which may well take some time. The knowledge requirements of the coach are also different as often the coach has no specific expertise to share except facilitation.

I find I spend most of my time at the non-directive end of this spectrum when I am coaching senior managers/executives. In such instances I am external to the client's organisation and know less than my coachee about the issues they face and how to do their job. Yes, I need to have a certain level of 'face validity' – in that both the client organisation and my coachee need to feel that I have worked at this level in an organisation and have the intellectual capacity to understand the issues they are facing – but I'm actually being hired for my coaching skills: my ability to get the coachee to work things out for themselves and come up with their own solution. In fact I always say I'm at my most 'dangerous' when coaching human resources professionals as that was my former career and I know a lot about the profession. At such times I'm conscious of reining myself back and not giving my coachee 'the answer' – which of course in most cases would simply be my version of the answer and not necessarily the 'right' answer.

For those new to coaching the idea of there being a coaching spectrum – and that, for much of the time, the best place for the coach to operate from on this spectrum is the non-directive end, thereby enabling the coachee to come up with their own solutions – often presents a real stretch. The urge to help the coachee out, give them the solution and hurry things along can be all too tempting. For many new coaches learning this first hand can be one of their biggest 'aha' moments. Just recently one of the coaches, Frances, on one of my ILM programmes shared such an insight with the group. Frances related how she had been working with one of her coachees and had suggested a couple of actions that she thought were obvious, but which he hadn't identified. She recalled how she noticed a 'real difference in impact'. When her coachee was coming up with his own ideas he wrote them in his book, and she'd been aware of him thinking and considering his options. However, when she made a suggestion the difference in his reaction was marked. He just acknowledged that Frances had spoken, wrote nothing in his book and effectively dismissed her ideas. Frances commented, 'I realised that he had thought of those suggestions, but they were not for him. I suggested them because to me they were the quickest route to his goal, but that was about my agenda and not his.'

In hindsight, Frances realised that she had been too directive and that her coachee needed to work out for himself his best course of action.

WHAT MAKES AN EFFECTIVE COACH?

Being able to navigate our way along the coaching continuum requires a blend of skills, knowledge and behaviour. One of the first activities I do on coaching skills workshops is to reflect on the characteristics of an effective coach. Not just someone who is an OK coach, or who does a bit of coaching when they can fit it in, but someone delegates would perceive to be a highly effective coach. In fact, someone they would want to be their coach. I'm careful to do this activity prior to providing input on 'good practice' from me so that delegates are working with their own views and experiences.

I ask delegates to split themselves into small groups and provide each group with a set of cards, each one with a different statement on it, and challenge them to select their top ten characteristics of an effective coach. Put another way, what would make the difference between someone who is a 'good' coach and someone who is a 'highly effective' coach?

Why not take a moment to complete the exercise for yourself – the statements are all provided below. List your top ten in table 1 at the end of this chapter. As you do so, think about why you think this particular characteristic is important.

- Creates time for coaching
- Actively listens to the coachee
- Builds rapport with the coachee
- Establishes what the coachee wants/needs
- Approachable/open
- Does what they say they'll do
- Shows a genuine interest in what the coachee wants to achieve
- Offers specific feedback about the coachee's behaviour/actions
- Summarises/paraphrases to check own understanding
- Asks the coachee for feedback on their performance as a coach
- Shares their own experiences with the coachee
- Accepts feedback/criticism from the coachee without becoming defensive/resentful
- Asks questions to get the coachee to explore issues more deeply
- Helps the coachee work things out for him/herself
- Avoids jumping to conclusions
- Is a sounding board
- Explores coachee's ideas without imposing own views

- Helps the coachee make sound choices
- Draws out understanding
- Offers alternative views
- Explains things clearly and succinctly
- Asks open questions (How? What? When?)
- Asks closed questions to focus on specific issue or get yes/no clarification
- Acknowledges the coachee's feelings: 'That must have been upsetting'
- Stimulates/fires the coachee's imagination
- Provides support
- Helps the coachee understand the effects of his/her behaviour on others
- Gets to the root cause of the problem
- Generates lots of different ideas
- Talks through problems/challenges
- Considers the likely consequences of different courses of action
- Explores the options – the pros and cons of different courses of action
- Is non-judgemental
- Is enthusiastic and provides encouragement
- Creates a safe environment for coaching
- Offers suggestions on possible solutions to problems
- Steers the coachee towards realistic courses of action
- Offers practical tips and techniques drawn from first-hand experience
- Encourages the coachee to take calculated risks/try different ways of doing things
- Helps the coachee identify/prioritise his/her development needs

- Encourages the coachee to take responsibility for his/her own learning and development
- Encourages the coachee to reflect on specific experiences in order to draw learning from them
- Enables the coachee to learn lessons from mistakes/setbacks
- Enables the coachee to learn lessons from successes/things that have gone well
- Encourages the coachee to have ongoing personal development plans

Of course, there is no definitive answer to this exercise and, to a large extent, your response will be determined by your own personal preferences, what you would value and your own view of good practice. However, having completed this exercise many times, I can now pretty much guarantee that groups will have six or seven of the same responses, including some of the following:

- Actively listens to the coachee
- Builds rapport with the coachee
- Establishes what the coachee wants/needs
- Shows a genuine interest in what the coachee wants to achieve

- Asks open questions (How? What? When?)
- Is a sounding board
- Is enthusiastic and provides encouragement
- Encourages the coachee to take responsibility for his/her own learning and development

Through discussion, delegates generally dismiss statements which they perceive to be too much about the coach's agenda in favour of ones which are really focussing on what the coachee wants and needs from the relationship and the coaching. 'Creates time for coaching' invariably provokes an interesting debate. Some groups argue that this is a given, whilst others point out that there is a big difference between making the time in your diary and showing up for sessions and really being 100% committed and focussed during coaching sessions.

Why not take a moment now and consider your current level of skill as a coach. For each of the ten characteristics that you have identified, rate your current level of competence, either using a scale of 1 to 10 or a traffic light system of red (area for development), amber (some level of skill) and green (good level of skill). I'd also invite you to review your self-assessment periodically as you continue your development as a coach.

EXERCISE – CHARACTERISTICS OF AN EFFECTIVE COACH

Table 1 My top ten characteristics of an effective coach

CHARACTERISTIC	MY CURRENT LEVEL OF COMPETENCE
1.	
2.	
3.	
4.	
5.	
6.	
7.	
8.	
9.	
10.	

Whatever you can do,
or dream you can,
begin it.
Boldness has genius,
power and magic in it.
Begin it now.

Goethe

CHAPTER TWO

GETTING READY TO COACH

As we have already explored, coaching can take various forms and, as a coach, we need to adjust our position along the coaching continuum depending on who we are coaching and the specifics of the situation. There may be times as a coach when I feel it is important to give some direct feedback on the impact my coachee is having on me right now as I believe this is a potential blind spot of theirs. There may be occasions when the most appropriate coaching intervention right now is to listen, really listen to what my coachee is telling me, including what their non-verbal behaviour is telling me which may not be articulated. Equally how I operate as a coach will also depend on how coaching fits with me. Is coaching something I do as part of my role as a manager or is it my full time job? My response to the above question will then influence how much 'getting ready to coach' I need to undertake.

If I'm a manager looking to utilise more coaching skills with my team, much of my coaching may be ad hoc or corridor coaching. By 'corridor coaching' I'm referring to spontaneous, unplanned coaching that takes place by a manager in response to a question from a member of their team. Rather than 'telling' the person the answer or how to address the problem, the manager adopts a coaching style – asking the individual what their outcome is, or what they would like to achieve, what options they have and which of these options they think is the best. This coaching is not planned and takes place on a day-to-day basis. Managers who ask coaching questions (see Chapter Four) rather than telling or providing answers are utilising a coaching style of management. If this is how I want to utilise coaching in my role there is probably very little preparation for coaching that I need to do. Coaching will be more about practising adopting a coaching style – i.e. asking coaching style questions, providing support, challenge, feedback and guidance in my day-to-day work.

As a manager, or internal workplace coach, I may also have more planned coaching sessions with team members, often as part of an ongoing development plan for an individual. For example, the individual may be seeking to develop their interpersonal skills or level of presence in meetings, presentations, etc. Planned coaching could also be used to help someone address a specific issue, for example conflict with another team member or work-life balance. This form of coaching is agreed between both coach and coachee and the coachee defines what they want to achieve. The purpose of the coaching is to help the coachee move forward and achieve their desired outcomes. The coaching may arise through a number of routes – requested by the coachee, suggested by the coach or as part of an ongoing personal development plan.

Since this form of coaching is agreed between the coach and coachee, to be really successful it does require the commitment of both parties. As the coach I need to be committed to the time the coaching is going to take which, certainly at first, is going to be longer than simply telling someone what to do. I need to be committed to practising coaching tools and techniques, which may feel different to my usual day-to-day modus operandi. I also need to believe in my coachee – that they have the innate ability and answers within themselves ultimately to achieve their outcomes. The commitment of the coachee to the process is also important, and the following are some useful questions to ask individuals who want to be coached.

DO YOU KNOW WHAT YOU WANT TO ACHIEVE?

A coachee may have an overall idea of what they want to achieve, for example, 'I want to get another job'. However, without real clarity about what this means in practice, the coaching will lack focus and may go off at a tangent. Chapter Five provides some useful questions to help coachees create well-formed outcomes for themselves prior to starting coaching.

DO YOU WANT TO CHANGE?

'Of course' is probably going to be a typical response and maybe I should change the above statement to 'Do you *really* want to change?' I have met a number of people over the years who have professed an interest in being coached. Perhaps they have had some feedback on their impact on others and how this could be more positive. However, as we have explored what coaching is, and what coaching isn't, it has become apparent that the individual's style is very much part of them. They are attached to it, they might even pride themselves in being a little different or 'quirky' and there is no real appetite to make any changes. They are coming to coaching because they feel they ought to, rather than because they really want to. In such circumstances the coaching is, at best, only going to be a partial success.

I recently completed an eight-week mindfulness programme as part of my own continuous professional development. At the end of the programme we were all asked to reflect on what was different for us. What were we doing differently? How had we changed? One of the delegates shared with the rest of the group some of the changes he had noticed in himself. As he did so he appeared quite perturbed. He continued, 'I came here expecting to learn some new things, to get some knowledge about mindfulness, but I didn't expect it to change me'. As I drove home, I thought just how relevant his comments were for coaching. Impactful coaching goes beyond simply learning new techniques and acquiring some new challenges. It challenges some of the beliefs we have about ourselves and our abilities, even our sense of who we are as a person and, through this process, we will change. As a coachee, are we truly up for that?

ARE YOUR EXPECTATIONS REALISTIC?

As a coach we genuinely need to believe in our coachees and their ability to achieve their goals, which is fundamentally not going to be possible from the outset if their expectations are totally unrealistic. Again the questions in Chapter Five are useful in encouraging a coachee to think through how realistic their goal is. Is it realistic to take on a general manager's role in two years or is that too big a stretch from where they are now?

ARE YOU WILLING TO TRY NEW THINGS?

There is a well-known phrase, 'If you always do what you've always done, you'll always get what you've always got' and this is so true for coaching. As individuals we all have some hard-wired habits. We've done things a certain way for years, which generally means that we get similar results. So, if we want different results then we need to adopt some different behaviours and practices and that can be a challenge. I often find would-be coachees have not necessarily made the connection between them wanting different results and them needing to try out some new things with, of course, no guarantee that these new things will work or bring out immediate success.

ARE YOU WILLING TO PUT IN SOME TIME AND EFFORT?

Woody Allen famously stated, '80% of success is showing up' and I think it's interesting to consider what it means to 'show up' from a coaching perspective. At a simplistic level this means turning up for coaching sessions and keeping pre-arranged times protected in the diary. Taken a stage further – what does it truly mean to 'show up' and be fully present in the coaching session? As we have already explored, coaching takes time and effort on the part of the coach. As a coach I want to feel that my coachee is equally committed. I often have a 'chemistry session' with potential coachees prior to commencing coaching, and during this session we explore what 'showing up' means for both of us and what steps we can take to facilitate this. For example, holding sessions either at the start or end of the day or avoiding having meetings immediately after sessions so there is time for reflection. For me, this level of commitment on both sides

29

is fundamental and I don't want to embark on a coaching relationship where commitment, from the outset, appears one-sided.

EMBEDDING THE LEARNING AND 'HOMEWORK'

Hawkins and Smith (2006) argue that if change 'doesn't happen in the room', i.e. during the coaching session, then it is not likely to happen. Whilst appreciating their sentiment here – coaches often refer to an 'aha' moment in coaching when all of a sudden the coachee 'gets it' – I don't agree that all of the learning during coaching does happen face to face with the coachee. I've certainly had a number of coaching sessions when I wondered how useful the session had been, how much had really resonated with the coachee, and how much they would take away and use, only to be surprised at the start of the next session when the coachee has told me just how useful the session was and what they have achieved since last time.

I also think that it is important that learning doesn't just happen 'in the room'. A coaching session can be a useful time to reflect, mull over something, take a different perspective on something, but, for me, it's not just about talking. As Blakey and Day (2012) put it, it can't just be about a 'cosy chat'; ultimately there has to be some action, putting these new insights into practice and seeing what happens.

For this reason I agree 'homework' with my coaching clients. It is part of our contract. We usually joke about it upfront, reminiscing about school homework and the 'dog ate my homework' excuse. But it's a serious commitment and is part of my coaching contract. I commit that if I say I will do something, be it sending my coachee some information, an article, some dates, etc., that I will do so. Equally my coachee commits that if they say they will do something then they do so or, if they don't for any reason, we will discuss why at the next session.

When I carried out my research for my Masters (outlined in more detail in the next chapter) I was interested that most of my coachees referred to agreeing 'homework' or tasks to undertake prior to their next coaching session. All saw these homework tasks as being fundamental to embedding their learning. Some of the ways in which 'homework' was set and agreed are described below.

PETER:

I tended to have a task to do, and then, 'How did you get on?' Lots of tasks were about conversations with people.

ADAM:

I'd have a task, and then there was the follow up in terms of, 'Did you do what you said you were going to do? How did that go? Did you present that? Did you present it the way you wanted to? Did you get over the message that you wanted?'

CHRIS:

Peter would write down three actions which we agreed and would then review progress at the next session. But that was a good discipline and I had something to come back to.

A pattern emerged of the majority of coaches agreeing homework tasks/actions with their coachees, although these may have been introduced quite casually, in the vein of 'why don't you try…?' However, the effect of these tasks appeared to be that their coachees went away and did something, tried something out, and this pattern of action, reflection, drawing conclusions and planning next steps helped embed the learning.

I've therefore developed a practice of agreeing 'homework' with my coachee at the end of a coaching session and then starting the next session with a review of this 'homework' from a standpoint of 'so, how did you get on...?'

ARE THEY PREPARED TO BE CHALLENGED/TAKEN OUTSIDE THEIR COMFORT ZONE?

This question links to some of the above themes and also brings in the concept of 'challenge' in the coaching relationship. How much challenge does the coachee want? How much are they up for? In Challenging Coaching, Blakey and Day explore the concepts of support and challenge in coaching. Support without challenge, they argue, can result in too many conversations taking place in the 'cosy chat' space.

I remember when I was starting out on my first coaching qualification many years ago being assigned a coach/ mentor, Mark, to work with during the programme. At our first meeting Mark asked me how I wanted him to work with me, to which I immediately responded that I wanted to be really challenged. This was the first qualification that I had done for a number of years and I wanted to get the most out of it. So, yes, I was up for a high level of challenge.

Mark smiled, and then asked, 'So, if you turn up one week and you've had a really bad week and you haven't done what you committed to do, do you still want me to really challenge you?'

I didn't even pause. 'No, of course not, I'd want you to be supportive if it was genuine.'

It's a conversation that has stuck with me and one which I have with my potential coachees. What level of challenge are they up for?

CAN YOU BE OPEN AND HONEST WITH ME?

As we'll explore in Chapter Three, so much of the success of coaching depends on the relationship between coach and coachee. So we need to agree right from the outset being open and honest with each other. In particular I emphasise the importance of the coachee being open and honest about our relationship, and if something isn't working – maybe they want less or more challenge or maybe they don't think they are really on track, but are reluctant to say so – that we have an open and honest conversation.

DO YOU BELIEVE THIS CAN WORK FOR YOU?

I think a number of caveats go along with this question. If someone is seeking coaching because they want to improve their self-confidence then they probably aren't going to be brimming with confidence about achieving their goal from the outset. They may also be carrying a number of limiting beliefs about what they are/aren't capable of based on previous experiences and things that they have been told in the past. That said, I would still want a good level of someone being 'up' for coaching, for really giving it their best shot, which can be tricky if someone has been 'sent' for coaching by their line manager. I therefore like to explore levels of commitment right at the start.

So far we have explored getting ready to coach through a lens of unplanned or planned coaching in a fairly informal and unstructured format. However, there will be occasions where we want to make our coaching more formalised. This could be when working as an internal workplace coach and will certainly be the case if we are working as an external coach. In such cases good practice would be to agree a coaching 'contract' or some ground rules right from the outset. Some of the areas you may want to discuss and agree are summarised below. This is not intended to be an exhaustive list, but will serve as a usual starting point.

What is my role as coach? This may appear somewhat obvious, but, as we discussed in Chapter One, people do have quite different perceptions of what coaching is. If I see my role as primarily operating from the non-directive end of the coaching spectrum then it's useful if I make this clear – especially if my coachee is expecting me to provide all the answers.

What is your role as coachee? Here I emphasise the importance of commitment, being open and honest and making the time for coaching.

Who sets the agenda? For me this is definitely the coachee and we always agree an agenda at the start of a coaching session. This agenda may, or may not, be what the coachee said they would like to explore at their last coaching session – something may have happened since our last session which they would now like to explore.

Coaching logistics. How frequently will we meet? How long will each session be? Where will we meet? (The coachee's place of work, my office, a coffee shop?) I don't have any hard and fast rules on location. If I'm meeting a coachee at their place of work, I do suggest that they try to choose a neutral space, for example a conference room, rather than their own office. This limits the chances of them being interrupted, and also means that there are less past experiences lingering in the room. For example, if the coachee has had a very difficult conversation with a team member just before his coaching session, the negative energy and emotions will still be present in the room, particularly if he is still sitting in exactly the same chair. So moving to a different space helps to signify that the coachee is moving into the coaching space. For me the key factors are that any environment needs to be comfortable for both coach and coachee with as few distractions as possible. Whilst coffee shops can be great places to meet, they aren't particularly private, and consideration should be given to aspects of confidentiality.

How long will our coaching relationship last? I've found that coaches have different views on this. Some are quite clear that there are a given number of sessions, and then, that's it, and I won't coach this person again. Others work with the same coachee for years. My own practice is to agree a defined number of sessions, invariably four to six, and be quite clear that our contract is for this number of sessions. Any additional ones would be the subject of a subsequent discussion once these sessions have been completed.

Confidentiality. Again this tends to be one of those terms that everyone uses, but with slightly different meanings. I think it is useful to be really clear upfront about expectations. I commit to all information in our sessions being completely confidential and remaining between us, i.e. the coach and coachee, unless:

- There is a life-threatening situation
- When required to impart information by law
- When working with my supervisor, at which time I would use only my coachee's first name and any corporate information would remain anonymous

There may also be occasions when confidentiality is an issue as outlined in the next point.

The role of the line manager or other third parties. Contracting can become more complicated if there is a sponsoring organisation paying for the coaching. The line manager and/or human resources may request feedback, perhaps a review part way through the coaching assignment, and often there is a final wash up session. In such cases it is useful to carry out three or four-way contracting upfront so that all parties are in agreement about how updates will happen, what will/won't be shared, etc. In addition I believe there is real benefit in having the line manager involved so they know what the coachee is working on and can provide opportunities for the coachee to practise new techniques and give feedback on any changes they have noticed. I therefore encourage the coachee to share learning with their line manager, and line managers to show an active interest so that the coaching is not taking place in a vacuum.

The boundaries – what's in and what's out? This aspect is about being clear what the coaching is for. Is this just about work, in which case anything outside of work should not be brought up or discussed, or is it life coaching and anything can be raised? Again I find different coaches have different views of this topic dependent on a variety of factors, including what brand of coaching they are offering, whether they tend to work with organisations who are paying for coaching or directly with individuals, and their own background and level of expertise. I tell my coachees to 'bring along the whole of you' as I believe if someone is having a difficult time in their personal life it will, in some shape or form, impact on their work life. So, for me it is acceptable to bring non work issues along. However, I am clear upfront about my own level of expertise. I'm not a counsellor, and I tell my coachees that, if I feel we are moving into territory that is not my area of expertise, I will say so. In practice this may involve assisting the coachee in finding alternative or additional support from a trained counsellor, etc.

The professional coaching bodies (the International Coaching Federation, Association for Coaching and the European Mentoring and Coaching Council) all have codes of practice which stipulate best practice around: levels of competence, managing boundaries, acting with integrity and professionalism. These codes are ones which coaches can adopt in their own coaching practice, and use as a starting point for contracting and touchstone if they feel they are facing an ethical dilemma.

What happens if it's not working? When I'm covering contracting on a training programme this point often provokes some discussion. Some feel that by raising this topic I'm putting 'this may not work' into the coachee's thinking. And I accept that this is a bit of a risk. However, I believe this is countered by a bigger risk that, if the coaching isn't working, the coachee won't say so. They may carry on half-heartedly, just going through the motions and seeing out the contract. Worse still, they may become too busy for coaching and stop the sessions. In both situations, as coaches we miss out on potential valuable developmental feedback for ourselves and the opportunity to get the coaching back on track. I therefore state upfront that if, for any reason, the coaching isn't working then either of us can cancel the coaching contract. However, in the spirit of openness and learning we commit to having a conversation with the other person giving our reasons why.

Passing on my experience/expertise. This may have been covered adequately under the first point, the role of the coach. There may be times, though, when you know that someone has specifically chosen you to be their coach because of your background. For example, 'I want to become an HR Director and you used to be one and that's why I selected you'. In such cases I would want an additional discussion about what the individual is expecting from me, and if and how I will pass on my expertise/experience if this becomes relevant.

Having discussed, and agreed upon, all of the above points I then summarise them in the form of a coaching contract which both parties sign and retain copies of. A short example coaching contract is reproduced at the end of this chapter.

From a sequencing perspective I usually find that I have met with (for example as part of a coaching chemistry session) or spoken on the phone with any new coachee and so we will already have spoken about what coaching is/isn't, what the coachee wants from coaching and the elements of the coaching contract. Once I receive confirmation that the coaching is going ahead I often send the coachee a copy of the contract so that this can be finalised at our first session. In addition I like to get my coachee to start thinking about what they want to get from coaching so they arrive at their first session having done some quality thinking and ready to start.

In the email confirming the date, time, venue of the first session, I therefore include the following (or very similar) words:

'Pre-Coaching Reflections

Coaching is very much about creating a reflective space and that may feel quite different for you if you're used to a fast pace of work. In readiness for this I feel it would be useful for you to spend some time ahead of our first session thinking about what you'd like to get out of this coaching.

In particular I'd suggest that you think about this in terms of:

- *What Do I Want To Achieve?*
- *How will I know I've been successful? Specifically, what will I be seeing? What will I be hearing? And what will I be feeling when I've achieved my outcomes?*
- *How Would You Like me to Work with you? What Would Bring Out the Best in You/Be Most Useful?'*

The final question links to a number of points that we've touched on in this chapter, particularly around commitment, level of challenge and taking personal responsibility. The reasons for the first two questions will become apparent in the following chapter.

In summary, there can be a number of steps to getting ready to coach. As a coach, making sure we take the time to do these properly ensures that we have some strong foundations in place for our coaching.

A SAMPLE COACHING CONTRACT

OUR COACHING COMMITMENTS

This following framework outlines some ground rules and commitments for our planned coaching sessions. The framework is intended to establish some principles and commitments from both me as the coach and you as the coachee.

My own role is to respond to your needs and agenda. You will be setting your own agenda. All our sessions will be confidential.

We will respect each other's time and other responsibilities and ensure that we do not impose beyond what is reasonable. Our coaching sessions will be approximately 1.5 hours in length with reasonable email and/or telephone contact in between sessions if needed by you.

We will be open and truthful with one another about the relationship itself, and I welcome constructive feedback on my performance as your coach.

As your coach I will encourage you to take responsibility and control of your own development. I will:

- Be reliable in keeping appointments
- Actively listen and help you explore your ideas without imposing my own
- Be non-judgmental
- Enable you to work things out for yourself

- Help you explore options and the advantages/ disadvantages of different courses of action
- Encourage you to reflect on specific experiences in order to learn from them
- Encourage you to set development objectives
- Provide constructive feedback as and when appropriate
- Enable you to establish what help, if any, you want/need and how you might access this.

In turn, I ask that you will:

- Make time for our coaching and mentoring sessions and be reliable in keeping appointments
- Complete tasks and homework assignments agreed in our coaching sessions
- Be honest and open in your conversations with me
- Focus on what you want (and not on what you don't want)
- Be 100% committed to taking responsibility for your own development.

THREE-WAY MEETING

As discussed, I would like to set up a three-way meeting between you, me and your line manager to agree some broad objectives for the coaching and engender (his/her) support in the process.

CONFIDENTIALITY

All the information from our sessions is completely confidential and will remain between us, except under the following circumstances:

1. There is a life-threatening situation
2. If required to impart information by law
3. When working with my supervisor, at which time I would only use your first name and any corporate information would remain anonymous.

I abide by the (name of organisation) code of ethics – a copy of which can be found at (website address)

Coach: …………………..   Coachee: ………………….

Date: ……………………   Date: ………………………

*We can make our minds so like still water
that beings gather about us that they may
see, it may be, their own images, and so
live for a moment with a clearer, perhaps
even with a fiercer life because of our
quiet.*

W.B. Yeats

CHAPTER THREE

CREATING THE COACHING SPACE

Several years ago I carried out some research as part of my Masters qualification in coaching and mentoring. I decided to focus on the sustainability of coaching. I was particularly interested in whether there was some form of 'honeymoon' period after coaching and, once this was over, coachees gradually returned to some of their previous practices, or whether the learning and change they had undergone was sustained. In addition, when learning/change had been sustained, what were the vital ingredients that had enabled this? As part of my research I interviewed a number of people who had all received coaching in the past, but had not received any coaching for at least six months. All claimed to have had a positive experience of coaching and my challenge was to identify the key ingredients that had made the coaching successful.

One area in which all the participants were in agreement was the importance of the coach/coachee relationship. It could be argued that this is a prerequisite of coaching and that any coaching assignment is likely to flounder if the relationship is not good. However, what also emerged was that, in successful assignments where the learning/change had been sustained, the coach/coachee relationship hadn't just been 'good' but 'excellent'.

There appeared to be a strong association between the strength of the coaching relationship and the level of sustainability post coaching. In addition, participants spoke of an excellent relationship that had formed right at the outset of the coaching, rather than one which had gradually developed during the course of the coaching.

During the interviews all participants were asked to complete the following sentence: 'The following ingredients are really important for sustained learning and change through coaching…' The response that was most frequently given by participants was 'trust'. Participants were then asked to expand on what they meant by 'trust' and why this was important to them. One interviewee, Adam, captured much of the participants' feelings around trust in the coaching relationship:

At a basic level you've got to absolutely trust the person because you do talk about stuff that you wouldn't normally talk about. I've spoken to Heather about stuff that I wouldn't talk to anyone else about – career and everything else. I think you need that level of trust to be able to really open up and make the most of it. If you're going to be identifying stuff around your weaknesses I think that's important.

During the interviews, all of the participants stressed the importance of having some kind of 'connection' with their coach. Most participants expressed this sense of 'connection' in terms of 'getting on', 'having a good sense of humour', 'gelling with the person' or there being a 'bond' or 'spark'. One participant, Andrea, provided a unique perspective on what it was like working with two different coaches. In recalling how she came to work with her second coach, she commented:

I did actually start off with another coach and I would not have been able to work with her. Through circumstances she moved on and Derek came along. But I knew I didn't have a connection with her. You do need to have a connection. A sense that they understand you.

For another participant, Oscar, 'connection' had a much deeper significance than simply gelling or bonding with his coach. His description of what it was like to have a 'connection' went right to the heart of what was really important to him; his beliefs and values. In recounting his first meeting with his coach, Mark, Oscar commented:

He resonated with what I was trying to get out of coaching. What I wanted to get out of the process... values and personal values and faith...and wanting to make sure that my values and faith were not over-presenting themselves. They infuse what I do. I spoke to Mark about this when we met – that side of things just resonated with Mark. The approach to people seemed to fit...

These findings echo those of previous research (Wasylyshyn, 2003; Thach, 2002; Bandura, 1994). Wasylyshyn used a quantitative approach with a survey sent to 106 coachees, enabling a broad range of issues to be addressed – coaching tools, reactions to working with a coach, factors in choosing a coach and the pros and cons of external versus internal coaches. The number one personal characteristic of an effective coach emerged as 'The ability to form a strong connection with the coachee', with 86% of respondents rating this as the key ingredient.

Carl Rogers's (1961) humanistic perspective similarly emphasises the attitudes and personal characteristics of the therapist and the quality of the client-therapist relationship as the prime determinants of the outcome of the therapeutic process. Rogers firmly maintained that people are trustworthy, resourceful, capable of self-understanding and self-direction and able to make constructive changes. It is the therapist's attitude and belief in the inner resources of the client that creates the therapeutic climate for growth. By being congruent, accepting and empathetic, the therapist is a catalyst for change:

If I can provide a certain type of relationship, the other person will discover within himself or herself the capacity to use that relationship for growth and change, and personal development will occur. (Rogers, 1961, p.33)

Corey endorses Rogers's comments from a coaching perspective

From a coaching standpoint the humanistic perspective suggests that, in contrast to the teacher or other expert role, the coach takes a less active and directive role. Interventions such as listening, accepting, respecting, understanding and responding must be honest expressions by the coach. Here, the focus of the coaching may be on working with the coachee to make them more aware of the ways in which they define themselves and their world and recognise the ways in which they are constricting their awareness and action, so they can see new alternatives for choice and action. (Corey, 2001, p.156).

My research, supported by reading and my own coaching practice, has brought home to me the importance of investing time and energy into developing a connection with your coachee. I was struck that no one I spoke to mentioned a fantastic tool or technique that their coach had used with them which had made a fundamental difference to them. The difference that made the difference was all about the importance of the coach/coachee relationship. We can refer to this as the 'connection' we make.

RAPPORT

Another term to describe this coach/coachee relationship, and one which is often used on coach development programmes, is 'rapport'. Rapport is about having a positive connection or affinity with someone. During a workshop, I often pose the following questions to get people thinking:

- What is rapport and how do you know you have it?
- If you were observing two people having a conversation, how would you know if they had a good rapport? What might you be seeing and hearing?

Most participants will answer the first question as a sense of feeling comfortable with someone, having a connection, feeling at ease, sharing the same values, a sense of both coming from the same place.

The second question tends to provoke some interesting discussion. At first participants will provide general comments: 'they will be chatting together and look comfortable'; 'they will be nodding'; 'they will look interested in each other'; 'they will both be laughing'.

As the discussion develops, people will get more specific about what they will be seeing and hearing. 'They will be making lots of eye contact'; 'their body language will be similar'; 'they will be matching and mirroring each other'; 'they will be using similar words/expressions or finishing off each other's sentences'.

Someone may even comment that the two people may in fact be saying very little, but you just know by looking at them that they are very comfortable in each other's presence. They do not need to talk to fill the silence.

As we continue to discuss rapport, participants will often talk about individuals they have known for years and how, when they meet up, it is as if they have never been apart. They are immediately on the same wavelength again. Conversely, others may recall how they met someone and they just clicked straight away – 'It was as if I'd known them all my life.'

I see some interesting examples of this instant rapport during coaching accreditation workshops.

I start by asking participants to provide some kind of introduction to themselves. A favourite involves choosing pictures from our extensive library of photographs which say something about them and where they are in their development as a coach. As the exercise progresses I notice that people will start to refer to other people's presentations: 'It really resonated with me what Julie said about...'; 'I nearly chose that photograph for exactly the same reason'; 'Well I also like to challenge myself and discover new things and I've chosen these photographs because...'

When debriefing the exercise, participants often volunteer how they felt a connection with someone because of something they said or did. Interestingly, when I ask people to choose a partner for the next exercise, individuals who have found an immediate connection gravitate towards each other.

BUILDING RAPPORT

As we explored in the previous section, if you are observing two people who are getting on very well together, you will notice that their body movements match or mirror one another.

As one person leans forward, the other will follow. If one person crosses their legs, the other soon does likewise. Where rapport exists, this happens quite naturally and spontaneously. It is also true, however, that if we consciously adopt the same sort of body postures as the other person (without obviously mimicking them) then we can build rapport and increase the receptivity of the other person without relying on a chance meeting of minds. The same is also true of voice quality and even breathing. If we start our conversation by matching the volume and pace of a person's voice then this builds a powerful sense of rapport at an unconscious level. There are four methods of gaining rapport:

MATCHING BODY POSTURES

The most obvious method, this entails subtly matching body postures, gestures and hand movements to support/emphasise communication.

MATCHING VOICE TONE OR TEMPO

Matching the other person's voice tone or tempo is a good way to establish rapport in the business world and an excellent method over the telephone when you are unable to see the other person. Tones can be soft or loud, high or low, fast paced or slow paced. Matching does not need to be exact – just close enough for the other person to feel understood.

MATCHING KEY WORDS/PHRASES

Using the exact words or phrases spoken by the other person, and even supporting these with matching gestures, will establish a sense of connectedness and rapport with the other person.

MATCHING BREATHING

Another method of establishing rapport, particularly effective when you cannot see the other person, is to match breathing rates. Once you have detected the other person's rhythm you can pace yourself into it. This is not as hard as it sounds as you can simply breathe in when the other person pauses in conversation and breathe out when they are speaking.

In all the above methods, once we have matched a person (match) and established rapport (pace) we can then change our voice or body language and the other person will follow us, i.e. we can lead. Leading is important because, if we change a person's external manner, we also alter their emotional or mental state. By first matching a person's posture and gestures and then changing our gestures to be (say) more open and relaxed, we could help to turn a more reserved coachee who is reluctant to contribute fully to one who will share some of their thoughts and observations.

When discussing the above Match-Pace-Lead rapport building model in a workshop I often give the following example: 'Imagine that at lunchtime I invite you all to go for a walk with me. We meet at the bottom of the stairs and I immediately set off walking very fast at 6.5km an hour. What would happen?'

Occasionally someone says that they would be up for the challenge and they would go along with me, and maybe even try and walk faster. However, most people freely admit that they would let me get on with it – they would either go at their own pace or give up, but they would not follow me at my pace.

I then ask, 'What would happen if, as we set off, I matched the general pace of the group at say 5km per hour (match) and walked at this pace for some time, ensuring that everyone was comfortably walking along with me (pace), and then gradually started to walk faster, say picking up the tempo to 5.5 or 6km per hour (lead)?'

The vast majority of people immediately volunteer that they would happily walk along with me and not even notice that I had picked up the tempo. If they did, they would probably only notice at the end when we stopped walking.

This for me is how true rapport building works. All too often rapport is seen as a quick 'Did you have a good journey here today?' before I turn to my business and attempt to lead you somewhere else. Building true rapport is about me taking time to make a connection, explore your world and match how you communicate (voice speed, volume, tone, expressions used, posture, gestures) before attempting to lead you elsewhere, maybe looking at a different way of doing something, taking a different perspective on something or challenging some of your limiting beliefs.

True rapport cannot be faked, and people sense when that connection is present. Charles expressed his connection with Peter as like that of a 'partnership'.

> *Peter was interested… he was interested in what I was doing, he wanted me to do well, it was like a partnership arrangement. There was an interest behind it, and that sort of 'yeah, I can't wait until the next session to see how you've got on'.*

I was intrigued and wanted to know more. The following extract continues Charles's account:

> Gill: *How could you tell he was interested?*

> Charles: *I think it was overall body language, his engagement, and when he summarised, he'd listened. He'd say, 'Let me see if I've got that right in my mind' and he'd play it back to me…and, on the whole, he was there. And at the next session he would remember what you'd discussed previously. And obviously he was taking notes as he went through, and half an hour before the session no doubt he was reading through them. But it was the engagement on the day in terms of taking an interest and not just asking the superfluous questions but asking the deeper questions in terms of 'I don't quite understand that, can you explain that to me?' so he could build up a complete picture in his mind. He could then try and picture the environment I was in and what I was facing. I think it's that deeper interest in questions rather than the stock answers.*

To develop your rapport-building skills practise some of the activities at the end of this chapter.

ACTIVE LISTENING

As highlighted above, building rapport with someone goes beyond simply copying their body language, tonality, etc. It requires a genuine level of interest in the other person and actively listening to what they have to say. Listening is much more involved and complicated than hearing, which is a physical process done with the ears. Besides hearing, listening also incorporates intellectual and emotional processes that together search for meaning and understanding. An effective listener listens not only to words but to the meanings behind the words. It is as if the listener possesses a 'third ear' that hears what is said without words, what is expressed soundlessly, what the speaker feels and thinks.

Effective listening is not a passive process. As a coach, when we are listening effectively, we are giving the coachee our full attention; 100% of our energy is focused on them and their message. We try to listen and understand every nuance, every word spoken, every message behind the words. We ask questions to clarify meanings if they are not clear to us. We lean forward in order not to miss anything. We maintain eye contact, nod or shake our head, we smile or frown. In other words, we make every effort to comprehend and our efforts are communicated back to the coachee by our nonverbal signs of attention and interest. Rapport and respect for our coachee have been established and maintained through the use of good listening skills.

By paying attention, we demonstrate respect for our coachee's thoughts, opinions, or concerns. They know that we are paying attention and that we are willing to assume value in what is being said. This does not necessarily mean that we always agree or understand, but it does show that we are tuned in and focused on the subject.

If you pick up a book on body language, chances are the book will refer to studies carried out by Albert Mehrabian in the mid to late 1960s on body language and non-verbal communication.

Mehrabian concluded that, when communicating feelings and attitudes, only 7% of meaning is directly taken from the words that are spoken. Mehrabian referred to 38% of meaning as being 'paralinguistic' (the way that the words are said, including tone, volume, rhythm, speed, pitch and clarity) and 55% of meaning as deriving from facial expression (eye contact, skin colour change, expressions).

Although this 7/38/55 ratio is widely presented as a communication truth, many have questioned how far the results from Mehrabian's study can be generalised. That said, I believe the essence of the model is powerful and helpful. The model certainly reminds us that it is dangerous to place undue reliance on words alone for conveying (sending and receiving) communications, especially those which carry potentially emotional implications.

We have all had the experience of listening and watching a politician speaking on television. The words are perfect, well-rehearsed and you cannot fault them. And yet, somehow you just do not believe them. Something about the voice tone or speed or the non-verbal expressions does not quite match up. In such situations we tend to believe the *signals* that we are picking up, rather than the *words*.

These additional non-verbal and verbal signals are often referred to as the 'meta message'. Meta is Greek for beyond. So listening at the meta-level means listening beyond the words. Skilled coaches have the ability to listen at the meta-level. They carefully check the non-verbal response against the verbal one to see whether they contradict or complement each other. This helps in developing assumptions, forming questions and confirming viewpoints. Skilled coaches also listen to how well the words they hear match with the tone of voice that they are said with.

We listen to different people in very different ways. Sometimes it's the individual who influences our degree of attention, sometimes it's the subject, sometimes external factors have an impact. It isn't easy to focus 100% of your attention on a speaker for very long, particularly if you are not accustomed to listening well. It requires an active effort to break the bad listening habits of many years. The following common situations illustrate how easy it is to stop listening effectively and become distracted during a coaching session:

- Wondering if you are over-parked, what time it is, being preoccupied with the phone call you took immediately before this coaching session, wondering how long it will take you to drive to your next appointment.
- Rehearsing your next question or wondering what activity to suggest doing with your coachee.
- Focusing on your coachee's typical expressions, mannerisms or gestures.

- Hanging on to every word with the intention of asking a question the moment your coachee pauses.
- Trying to write down every word your coachee is saying.

In *Time to Think*, Nancy Kline refers to a quality of attention and listening which succeeds in promoting 'generative thinking'. Nancy argues that the human mind wants attention, and that, for the most part, we experience breakthroughs when we are with another person. Nancy advocates building a 'thinking environment' where there is time and space to think – 'ease' as opposed to rush – our attention and tone says 'you matter' and the key focus of listening is on generating independent thinking in another person. Nancy's Thinking Pairs work involves asking two simple questions:

The opening question 'What do you want to think about and what are your thoughts?'

With the follow up question 'What more do you think, feel or want to say?' if the thinker runs out of thinking.

It is a different way of coaching and a great way of honing your listening skills and ability to listen with all of your attention.

One aspect that I find novice coaches often struggle with is silence. In everyday conversations there is typically very little silence. At best one person talks and then the other person talks. In reality there are probably large portions of time when both are talking and interrupting each other and very little true listening is going on. The same is true when we ask a question. Our natural reaction if the person does not answer immediately is to fill the silence – answer the question for them, rephrase it, ask another question. Highly effective coaches have the ability to ask a question and give the coachee time and space to think about their answer and respond in their own time. They have overcome their discomfort with silence. Nancy Kline argues that silence is at the core of the thinking environment and that much of what is generative is silence – mostly from the listener (the coach), but often from the thinker (the coachee). So listening, real, active listening, the kind of listening that says 'I'm truly interested in you and what you have to say', together with the ability to hold a silence whilst you think something through for yourself, is, I would argue, one of the fundamental skills that we need to develop to be an effective coach.

TIPS FOR DEVELOPING EFFECTIVE LISTENING SKILLS

There are several principles and techniques that can help you to listen better. It must be stressed, however, that the only way to break bad listening habits is through the practice, practice, and more practice of good listening habits. Like driving a car, you learn theory in the classroom sessions, but it is hours of practising on the road that allows you to develop the necessary skills to acquire your driver's licence. The following techniques require the same attention.

Learn to recognise your personal signals that your attention is wandering (i.e. doodling, thinking about other things, glancing at your watch, leaning back in your chair).

When your attention wanders, consciously bring it back and refocus on your coachee (this will happen frequently until you become more skilled).

Position yourself where you are least likely to be distracting by noise, views and people. Stay focused on your coachee.

Practise initially suspending judgement or preconceived notions and simply listen to what your coachee has to say.

If you lose focus (if appropriate) admit it and ask questions to regain focus.

Whenever possible, reflect back the content and feeling of the coachee's message and listen to the speaker's reaction for confirmation or clarification of your understanding. Practise using clean language (see Chapter Four). This is a fantastic way to develop listening skills.

Give signs of nonverbal attention and interaction. Lean forward, look at the speaker, don't fidget.

Practise attentive listening. Give your coachee your full attention. Lean forward, look at them, don't fidget, resist the temptation to make lots of active listening sounds and gestures – nods, 'uhmms', 'yes', etc. – forget taking notes and just listen.

Levels of listening exercises are provided at the end of this chapter.

I had just starting working with a new coachee, Lisa. Lisa had been acting up in a role for a year, but her application for the role on a permanent basis had been unsuccessful. We'd met for a chemistry session and then for a three-way contracting session with her Director. Whilst Lisa had been positive at both she'd been reticent and, I felt, guarded. Her body language suggested that there was a lot that she was feeling but not articulating. When she said that she was 'comfortable' with the situation she looked anything but comfortable. I sensed that it would take some time for her to open up.

At our first session I focussed my attention on creating a coaching presence and making a real connection with Lisa, heart to heart.

I asked Lisa what she wanted to get out of the coaching sessions. As she started to answer she broke down in tears. I held the silence and nodded as encouragement for her to continue. Between sobs my coachee poured out her feelings – shame at having to tell her family and husband that she'd been unsuccessful, relief as she hadn't enjoyed the role and knew she'd been struggling and finally a huge sense of personal failure in not managing to secure the role. I asked if she'd shared these feelings with anyone else, to which she just shook her head and said no.

I sensed that this was an important moment for Lisa and that she needed time and space to express her feelings. I remained silent but fully present. For the next thirty minutes I listened with my whole body whilst she relived the range of emotions she'd experienced, crying throughout. Eventually the tears subsided, she dried her eyes and gave me a wan smile.

'So what would you like to happen?' I asked her.

Without hesitation, she replied, 'It was the right decision, I was too young, too inexperienced, it was too big a stretch. But I want to be ready for that role next time round. That's what I want.' We spent the final ten minutes of the session creating some outcomes for the coaching, after which she reapplied her makeup and left my office. At our next session she appeared focussed and smiling and ready to start. The tears never reappeared.

If you are an inexperienced coach reading this you may be wondering how you will cope if strong emotions arise during your own coaching sessions. I've worked with a number of coachees who have had painful experiences, but haven't subsequently reflected on these experiences and their feelings and emotions arising out of these. And they certainly haven't shared these feelings and emotions with anyone else, and so starting to share can open the floodgates.

From a purely practical perspective I would recommend having a box of tissues close by just in case. In addition, as I described in the above scenario, allow time and space for your coachee to express and explore their emotions. Recognising and naming the emotion(s) involved can be an important step to moving forward. Being aware of the potential for such reactions is the first step to handling emotionally charged situations.

EXERCISES – LEVELS OF LISTENING

Our ability to listen, to let go of our own agenda and focus 100% on someone else's words, message and unspoken words, is a key skill for building rapport. If we can pick up on what is important to someone we can skilfully package our own ideas so they dovetail. Try the following levels of listening with a partner to gain an appreciation of what it is like to listen actively and develop your skill.

EXERCISE – LISTENING AT LEVEL 1, CHATTING WITH RAPPORT

Decide who will be the speaker and who will be the listener. The speaker's role is to talk about a recent experience, e.g. a holiday, hobby, project at work.

The listener's role is to listen to the words and interpret the story in terms of your own experience. Make frequent comments offering your own opinion and sharing your *own* experiences.

Think about how you would have done it differently or how you might improve on what your colleague did.

After five minutes or so share what it was like to listen at Level 1, and to be listened to. What was going on for each of you at the time? After a short debrief, change roles.

EXERCISE – LISTENING AT LEVEL 2, CURIOUS LISTENING

The speaker's role is to talk about a different story.

The listener's role is to:

- Get into rapport with your partner (matching and mirroring body language, matching posture, maintaining eye contact, matching tone/volume/speed).
- Ask questions to clarify and seek more information.
- Summarise/reflect back/paraphrase.
- Be curious. Show by your body language that you are interested in them and their story.
- Be alert for your partner's values as they are expressed in the story – what is important to your partner?
- Stay completely focussed on your partner by listening and responding at Level 2. Do not add any opinions or views of your own.

After five minutes or so share what it was like to listen at Level 2, and to be listened to. What was going on for each of you at the time? How was the experience different from listening at Level 1? After a short debrief, change roles.

I keep six honest serving men
(They taught me all I knew);
their names are What and Why and When
And How and Where and Who.

Rudyard Kipling.

CHAPTER FOUR

QUESTIONS, QUESTIONS, QUESTIONS

As human beings we are programmed to answer questions. If I ask you a question, for example 'What was the name of your first teacher?' or 'What is your first memory of a holiday?', you may not immediately know the answer to this question. However, your curiosity has been aroused. Sometime later – perhaps when you are shopping in the supermarket or soaking in the bath – you will no doubt remember. 'Of course. It was Mrs Rowson.' Our unconscious mind has kept working on the problem and eventually retrieved the answer.

The ability to ask questions – questions that really provoke thought – is a core skill of coaching. Having run many coaching accreditation programmes over the years and spoken to numerous people who have been coached, either by myself or someone else, I hear the same thing time and time again. How the process of being asked questions has become ingrained in the individual and how they now use these techniques with others, generally without conscious thought. One person recently commented:

> *All the way along I think the thing that helped was that Robert, my coach, wasn't there to give advice, wasn't there to guide me, he was there to ask questions, and I guess over the twelve months he's ingrained some of*

those questions in my mind that I use for myself and with managers reporting to me. Just being able to probe and ask questions and not jump in with a solution for them, but to help them think through in their own mind.

Referring back to the Spectrum of Coaching Skills, introduced in Chapter One and which is reproduced below, we can see that all of the non-directive or pull techniques make significant use of questioning.

However, the purpose of the questioning may be quite different. Questions to raise awareness have a different purpose to questions which are simply aimed at helping the listener understand the speaker. In this chapter we will explore a range of questions that we can use in coaching, from 'clean' questions, where our only agenda is to help the coachee really understand their issue, to powerful and incisive questions where our focus is on raising the coachee's awareness, perhaps around some of the limiting beliefs they are holding about themselves

Figure 2 The Spectrum of Coaching Skills

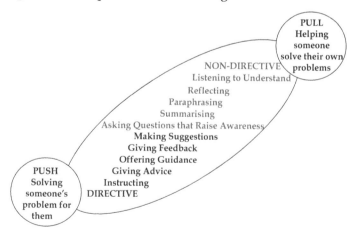

66

and/or to challenge our coachee into thinking about other options or a potential solution to their issue.

SEEKING INFORMATION AND TESTING UNDERSTANDING

One of the simplest ways of ensuring that you have understood what your coachee is saying is asking questions. For example, it is the first meeting with your new coachee, they have just spoken at length about their issue, used lots of three letter acronyms and names of people you do not know and their thoughts are jumbled as they seek to tell you all their story. You are having difficulty following their train of thought and sorting out the issues and feel overwhelmed and confused. In this situation we will be asking questions to clarify our coachee's meaning and/or to confirm our understanding.

Clarifying questions are useful to ensure that we have clearly understood what our coachee has said. At times we may want our coachee to expand on their comments, sometimes we may simply not follow the line of reasoning and ask questions to help us comprehend. Clarification of what we hear demonstrates our respect and willingness to listen. Crucially, from a coaching perspective, it also shows interest and empathy. Clarifying questions do not mean, however, that we necessarily agree with what is being said. Rather they help to ensure that coach and coachee have a shared understanding of the goal or issue.

Confirming questions serve a slightly different purpose in effective communication and coaching. Typically we ask for confirmation once we are confident that we have fully understood the message being sent. In a sense, we are confirming our understanding as a coach and receiving an acknowledgement from the coachee that we have indeed captured the essence of the message and can move on to the next step. The next step may be a deeper discussion of the issue or it could mean closing that particular area and moving on to another. Equally, the response to our confirmation may indicate that we did not understand fully and we may need to clarify further.

Ask clarifying questions to get to the meaning behind the words.

Ask confirming questions to make sure you have understood.

OPEN AND CLOSED QUESTIONS

Broadly speaking there are two types of questions we can ask. Open questions encourage the speaker to expand on an idea or give further details. Open questions typically start with 'What', 'Where', 'When', 'Why', 'Who' and 'How'.

In coaching our focus tends to be on asking open questions so we can elicit more information from our coachee, acquire a deeper understanding of the subject being discussed and, crucially, enable the coachee to gain a clearer understanding of the real issues and opportunities by talking them through and reflecting on them at a deeper level. Asking open questions can present a challenge to time-pressed managers who have become used to hearing a question or problem and quickly supplying a solution. Taking time to explore the issue further through asking open questions can, certainly in the short term, feel like a waste of time. It is quicker to supply the solution. However, in the long term asking questions promotes a climate of getting people to think through issues for themselves and more sustained learning. As one leader who had received some coaching recently said to me:

One thing I've really learned is the power of asking open questions. Today I'm much more likely to ask, 'How do you think you should tackle it?' or 'What makes you say that?' Previously if someone came to me with an issue I tried to solve it.

Some examples of open questions:

'What are you going to do next?'
'What options are available to you?'
'Who could help you with this?'
'How will you know you've been successful?'
'What do you feel is the real issue here?'

At this point, when I'm running coach training sessions, I mention that the least useful open question to ask, from a coaching perspective, is 'why'. This invariably provokes a response. Delegates argue that the 'why' question is very useful. 'Isn't it useful to know exactly why someone feels or acts in a certain way?' Yes, it can be, and 'why' is an incredibly useful question. It is probably the first question we learn as a child and repeatedly ask during our formative years as we start to make sense of the world. In business it is a question we repeatedly ask as we attempt to understand why things have gone wrong or problem-solve using root cause analysis. However, the problem with 'why' is that it can sound accusatory or parental. Consider the question 'Why did you do that?' If I am feeling unsure of myself and my actions I can easily answer the question by trying to justify my actions.

In addition, for the coach 'why' can be a particularly unhelpful question. Consider the following exchange:

Coachee: *I've always been hopeless with any form of new technology.*

Coach: *Why do you say that?*

Inadvertently the coach has now given the coachee a great platform to vocalise all the reasons why they believe themselves to be hopeless with new technology.

Coachee: *Well I was absolutely useless with any kind of electronic toy as a child, it took me ages to learn to use a computer, and as for my phone, I probably only use a couple of the features. And now I've been given an iPad at work...heaven knows what they expect me to do with that...You see...I'm absolutely hopeless. Always have been.*

Has the 'why' question helped the coachee or moved them on in their thinking? I would argue no, and that it has, in fact, succeeded in helping the coachee dig themselves into an even bigger hole. They have now reinforced their belief that they are hopeless with new technology. So, 'why' is the one question that I encourage coaches to use sparingly. Most 'why' questions can be asked using 'what' or 'how' instead. For example:

Coachee: *I've always been hopeless with any form of new technology.*

Coach: *What leads you to that conclusion?* or *How have you come to that conclusion?*

The other type of question is a closed question that effectively limits a response to a simple yes or no, the selection of an alternative, or an exact amount. Closed questions often contain words like 'how many/much/ often…', 'which do you prefer?', 'are you saying that…', 'does this mean that…', 'do you…'. Such questions do not encourage expansive responses, and therefore in coaching we tend to avoid asking too many closed questions. However, closed questions can be useful to help narrow down options, confirm understanding, seek specific details and provide more concrete focus to a discussion. Some examples of closed questions:

'How often do you have these thoughts?'
'How many times have you told him?'
'Does this mean that you are going to say no
to this request?'
'So which option are you going to choose?'
'So you will do that by Monday?'

POWERFUL COACHING QUESTIONS

So far I have focussed on questions with the intent of listening and understanding where the coachee is coming from. However, as coaches there will be times where we ask questions with the specific intent of raising awareness and prompting the coachee into taking some form of action. Our aim is to ask tough/challenging/ powerful questions to make our coachee think. Another former coachee relived with me an experience of being asked some tough or powerful questions by his coach:

Being put under the spotlight, attention on me…not just asking questions, asking lots of questions, questions on top of questions. Questions about the answers you've given. That for me is quite thought provoking. Managers will generally ask questions, but accept the answer you give. Powerful coaching questions dig a lot deeper…

Powerful coaching questions have the following characteristics:

- They are usually open questions – starting with 'who', 'what', 'when', 'where' and 'how'. (As mentioned above, use 'why' sparingly and with care.)
- They refocus thought, for example from problem to solution, from past to future.
- They tap into creativity and create options.
- They make a problem feel more like a challenge or opportunity.
- They make helpful assumptions. For example:
  - What other choices do you have? (Assumption – you have more than one choice.)
  - What were you trying to achieve from that? (Assumption – you were trying to achieve something. You didn't deliberately set out to mess up.)
  - What will you do differently next time? (Assumptions – there will be a next time and you will do something different.)
  - What is good about the current situation? (Assumption – there is always something good. You may just have to dig a little to find it.)
  - Tell me about a time when it went well for you. (Assumption – there has been a time when it went well for you.)
  - What advice would you give to a friend in your position? (Assumptions – you have some advice to give and you have at least one friend.)
  - If you knew the answer, what would it be? (Assumption – deep down you know the answer to this problem.)

Several years ago I was running a Presenting Yourself with Impact workshop for one of our global clients. There were twelve delegates at the workshop and, although it was being conducted in English, this was the second language for many of them. On the second day all of the delegates delivered a presentation and received some feedback from their peers and the facilitators, after which we held a final wash up session. One of the delegates, who was Italian, asked a question:

'I received feedback that my presentation lacked structure and I'm wondering if it's because I was delivering the presentation in English, my second language'.

My colleague, who had heard his presentation, asked him, 'What do you think?' to which he replied 'I don't know'.

My colleague paused and then asked him, 'If you knew the answer to that question what would it be?'

The delegate did not even stop and think. He immediately replied, 'Oh it would be exactly the same. I am unstructured!'

A simple example and one that has stuck with me. How often do we, or others, hide the answer from ourselves? Maybe the answer we have is somewhat unpalatable or difficult and we are rather hoping that we will be given a 'better' answer by someone else. Maybe it is just easier to ask someone else than take the time to work through the answer ourselves. So this question can be a very powerful coaching question. However, use it sparingly – if you constantly bat questions back with a glib sounding 'If you knew the answer what would it be?' you will frustrate people.

Here are some examples of powerful questions in action:

Coachee's statement: *I want to go on a training course, but I've been told it's too expensive. It's not fair.*

Coach's powerful question: *How can you achieve your learning objective another way?*

Coachee's statement: *I've twice applied for a new role and been runner up on both occasions. The situation's just impossible.*

Coach's powerful question: *What could you be doing to make sure you're the first choice candidate next time?*

Now have a go at the following examples. Beside each of the coachee's statements/problems write down some powerful questions. Try to think of three or four questions for each statement/problem. Think beyond the obvious questions.

- I can't do anything about it.
- I'm useless at this.
- I've been stuck in this job for too long.
- I can't do that.
- An example of your own.

PRECISION QUESTIONS

Sometimes when we are coaching others we notice patterns of thinking or behaviour in how the coachee uses words that suggest they are stuck in a particular way of thinking. Here precision questions, sometimes also referred to as incisive questions, can be useful in highlighting to the coachee the 'trap' that they are in and encouraging the coachee to escape from the 'trap'. I find that four of these patterns/traps occur quite frequently in coaching: Universals, Comparators, Imperatives and Limiters. I will deal with each of these in turn, explaining the trap, the precision questions that can be used and providing some examples for you to have a look at yourself. Precision questions should be used with care, and only when rapport has been built or they can be received as too blunt or 'gotcha' questions with the coach trying to be clever. Used sparingly and with rapport they can be a great way of highlighting a pattern of thinking that the coachee has got stuck in.

IMPERATIVES

Imperatives are where the coachee uses words such as 'must', 'should', 'have to', 'ought to'. For example, 'I have to work very long hours.'

We can challenge this thinking with two different kinds of precision questions. 'What makes it necessary?' to find out the reasons, or 'What would happen if you didn't?' to get the outcome. Try formulating precision questions for the following statements:

- 'I must stay late to complete this task.'
- 'She should know better.'
- 'I have to get this report out by Friday.'
- 'I ought to say I'm not happy with the decision.'

COMPARATORS

Comparators are where the coachee uses words such as 'more', 'less', 'better', 'worse'. For example, 'I could do better'.

We can challenge this thinking with two different kinds of precision questions. 'Better than what?' to get to the basis of the comparison, or 'How much better?' to get the outcome. Try formulating precision questions for the following statements:

- 'His instructions need to be clearer.'
- 'He needs to listen to me more.'
- 'She needs to talk less.'
- 'I could organise things better.'
- 'The situation is getting worse.'

UNIVERSALS

Universals are when the coachee uses words such as 'every', 'each', 'all', 'none', 'never', 'no one'. For example No one understands me'.

We can challenge this thinking with two different kinds of precision questions. 'Are there any exceptions?' to find out if the statement is true, or simply to repeat and stress the universal to search for exceptions. For example:

Coachee: *No one understands me.*

Coach: *No one?*

Try formulating precision questions for the following statements:

- 'She's always miserable.'
- 'No one trusts him.'
- 'Everybody dislikes him.'
- 'She never returns my calls.'
- 'He turns down every request for resources.'

LIMITERS

Limiters are where the coachee uses words such as 'can't' or 'impossible'. For example, 'I can't say no to her'.

Again, we can challenge this way of thinking by asking two different kinds of precision questions. 'What prevents you?' to get to the reason and 'What if you did?' to get to the outcome. Try formulating precision questions for the following statements:

- 'It's impossible to ask for help.'
- 'I can't do anything about it.'
- 'You couldn't say what you really think in a meeting.'
- 'It's impossible to get him to change his mind.'

SUMMARISING/PARAPHRASING/REFLECTING

The next series of interventions on the Spectrum of Coaching Skills are summarising/paraphrasing and reflecting. Broadly speaking these are all techniques to promote mutual understanding by restating what has been said in our own words and then seeking confirmation of our comprehensions, usually with a closed question. When we summarise/paraphrase/ reflect we are demonstrating to the coachee that we want to understand clearly and precisely what they are saying. In addition, summarising/paraphrasing/reflecting are invaluable practices for a developing coach as they compel us to listen; let the coachee know that we are aware and understand what they are saying; and help create empathy and rapport. Equally we are providing an opportunity for the coachee to hear their message, and even words, spoken back and reflect on whether that is really what they mean; is there more that needs to be said; is there something else going on here? The closed question at the end of our reformulation invites the coachee to agree with our understanding, or to clarify any points. For example:

'So you're saying that you've been in this role now for three years, you're feeling a bit bored, not particularly stretched by the work you're doing and you feel ready for a new challenge. But you're not sure what that next challenge is yet'. (Reflecting understanding)

'Is that correct?'
(Closed question to confirm)

Summarising/Paraphrasing/Reflecting share the same core purpose – restating what has been said and then seeking confirmation of this from the other person. However, they do have some key differences.

Summarising. When we summarise we focus on adding up all the issues and/or feelings and restating these with the purpose of serving as a check point for further discussion. For example, 'These are the key issues you expressed', 'If I understand how you feel about…'

Paraphrasing. Paraphrasing is similar to summarising in that it focusses on not introducing any new subjects or topics, and the coach will typically use a lot of their own words. A paraphrase is likely to be longer than a summary, but the coach will still use fewer words than the coachee they are paraphrasing.

Reflecting. Reflecting involves much more use of the coachee's own words than paraphrasing. Here the coach is deliberately reflecting back to the coachee what they have just said, including any feelings they have expressed. For the coach this involves a much deeper level of listening – the specific words the coachee has used, changes in non-verbal behaviour, expressed or suppressed feelings – listening with the eyes as well as the ears. As such, reflecting allows a more complete understanding (thoughts and feelings), going beyond a superficial understanding of the issues and demonstrating empathy.

CLEAN QUESTIONS

The most non-directive intervention on the Spectrum of Coaching Skills is listening to understand. Here the coach is simply listening with the primary purpose of understanding where the coachee is coming from. Equally the coach might choose just to listen and ask very few questions with the purpose of allowing the coachee to explore their own thoughts and ideas with as little contamination from the coach as possible. When trying to illustrate what it means simply to listen as a coach I invariably introduce people to clean language.

Clean language involves keeping your own language and experiences out of your questions. The clean language technique emerged during the 1980s in the work of the New Zealand therapist, David Grove. In the early 1990s two NLP trained therapists, James Lawley and Penny Tompkins, became very interested in Grove's work and curious to find out exactly how he did what he did. Over a number of years they spent a good deal of time observing Grove at work, culminating in their book, *Metaphors in Mind*, which now provides one of the main sources of information about clean language.

A clean language conversation is very different from an everyday conversation. When using clean language everything you do or say is intimately related to what your coachee says and does. The entire focus of the process becomes an exploration of the coachee's model of the world from their perspective, using their sense of time and space and using their words. Whilst in everyday conversations the quality of a question is generally judged by the information it elicits and how useful that is to the questioner, with clean language the quality of the question depends on how the coachee processes the question and how useful it is to them. By way of illustration I often share the following transcripts of two different coaching conversations. I explain that, prior to the coaching conversation taking place, the coachee had identified that they were struggling to find their own work-life balance and had been asked by the coach to find a metaphor to describe their current sense of being out of balance.

Take a moment to read both coaching conversations. In both cases the coachee and their issue are identical, but the approach taken by the coach is different.

COACHING SCENARIO 1

Coachee: *The metaphor is a roller coaster.*

Coach: *A roller coaster. Why a roller coaster?*

Coachee: *Well there're two extremes. There's a good part which is very energising and the other part which is a kind of sinking feeling.*

Coach: *I see, a roller coaster with a good part and a bad bit?*

Coachee: *Yes, well sort of – an energising part and a part which is sinking…I'm not sure it's altogether bad. But there's a difference.*

Coach: *Actually, which is the good part – when you're climbing to the top or when you've just started the descent? I know which one it is for me. I love the bit when you've just gone over the edge and you know your stomach is about to flip…*

Coachee: *Oh, I hate that…at that moment I feel so out of control. Not sure what it is for me. I like the bit of almost* *being at the bottom and knowing the worst is over. Maybe I've chosen the wrong metaphor. Maybe there's a better one. I'm not sure…*

Coach: *Well, let's stick with the roller coaster for now. So, what are your feelings towards this roller coaster?*

Coachee: *Feelings?* (pauses) *Somewhat confused, I guess. Some parts of it are very attractive. They're exciting, exhilarating. Whilst other parts are more draining.*

Coach: *Hmm, a roller coaster sounds a good metaphor for this. Let's stick with the fun parts. Can you describe them in a bit more detail?*

Coachee: *Well, there's an energy and excitement.* (pauses) *Not sure what else I can say really. The sinking feeling is never very far away.*

Coach: *OK, so that part is kind of lively and fun and you like it. So let's look at the bad part of the roller coaster. Can you describe your feelings in a bit more detail?*

Coachee: *It's a mixture of feeling tired and a sinking feeling of 'here we go again'.*

Coach: *So no energy, feeling drained, can't be bothered…*

Coachee: *Not that I can't be bothered. I can. I recognise it's a pattern and there's a sense of going back there and not wanting to, but I don't feel I have the energy to do something different.*

Coach: *So you've got a roller coaster with a good part and a bad part and you're being pulled back to the bad part. So let's focus on the good part. This fun, energetic part. What have you tried so far?*

Now read through the second coaching scenario noticing the different style of coaching.

COACHING SCENARIO 2

Coachee: *The metaphor is a roller coaster.*

Coach: *A roller coaster. And is there anything else about that roller coaster?*

Coachee: *There are extremes in the roller coaster. Some parts are very exhilarating, very energising and just feel really good. And the other extreme is a kind of sinking feeling, of being slightly out of control.*

Coach: *So, a roller coaster…and extremes…and exhilarating, energising and a sinking feeling and out of control…?*

Coachee: *Yes.*

Coach: *And when it's a roller coaster with extremes, where is that roller coaster?*

Coachee: *It's in here.* (puts hand on stomach)

Coach: *It's in here?* (puts hand on stomach)

Coachee: *Actually it's not…Some of it is here* (points to chest) *and some of it's here* (points to stomach). *The good bits are here* (chest) *and the sinking feeling's here* (stomach).

Coach: *And the good bits are here* (chest) *and the sinking feeling is here* (stomach). *And is there anything else about those good bits here?* (chest)

Coachee: *Yes. There's an energy to it. And as I'm describing it to you now I can feel that. It's a positive energy.*

Coach: *And is there anything else about that positive energy you can feel?*

Coachee: *Yeah. There's something about focus and drive and things being good and feeling OK.*

Coach: *And focus, drive and feeling good and things being OK?*

Coachee: *And it's about kind of being in the moment and experiencing that for what it is.*

Coach: *And what kind of moment is that moment when you're being in the moment?*

Coachee: *It's a moment when things feel good and have a sense of balance and it's a paradox because there's energy, but there's also a sense of calm as well.*

Coach: *So there's energy and calm and a sense of balance. And what kind of balance is that balance?*

Coachee: *It's like a seesaw.*

Coach: *Like a seesaw?*

Coachee: *Yes. In that it feels right and it does balance and it goes backwards and forwards.*

Having read out both scenarios I then ask delegates what they noticed about the two scenarios. Delegates comment immediately that in the first scenario the coach used a lot of their own language and own assumptions. For example the coachee's statement 'There's a good part which is very energising and the other part which is a kind of sinking feeling' is rephrased by the coach as 'A roller coaster with a good part and a bad bit'. The coach also makes an assumption as to the 'other part' based on their own experience. By contrast, in the second scenario the coach uses the coachee's own words and gestures rather than paraphrasing or rewording. They add no thoughts or ideas of their own. The coach's job is to direct the coachee's attention in fresh ways and to be an attentive listener to whatever emerges.

Having immediately spotted the key differences between the two scenarios, someone will invariably comment, 'Yes, but it would drive me mad if someone coached me like that and parroted back what I'd just told them.' And I understand what they mean. Clean language is deliberately very repetitive and in everyday conversation would sound very strange. However, used skilfully in a suitable setting, the experience for the coachee is of attention being focused and of being given space to think and explore.

In the second scenario much use is made of Lawley and Tompkins's nine basic clean language questions. Their model is reproduced in figure 3.

So you are probably wondering why I am introducing clean language if I am also admitting that it can sound repetitive and strange. I do so for three key reasons. Firstly I find that people consistently over estimate how 'clean' they are with their questioning and are unaware of how many of their own preferences, assumptions, beliefs and thoughts leak into their coaching. The first scenario using 'dirty' language rather exaggerates this point, but the overall message is received and understood. Once delegates start doing their own coaching they appreciate at first hand the impact of using their own words instead of the coachee's. I often hear feedback along the lines of 'Your questions were a bit dirty' or 'You used a different word to the coachee and I noticed how it jarred with them'. Secondly, the basic clean language questions are great questions In particular 'Is there anything else about X?' and 'What kind of X is that X?' are questions that I use frequently in my own coaching practice. In addition, the questions are all softly prefaced with 'And'. I often say to trainee coaches, 'If in doubt, or if you really don't know what to ask next, say

Figure 3 The Nine Basic Clean Language Questions 'Compass'

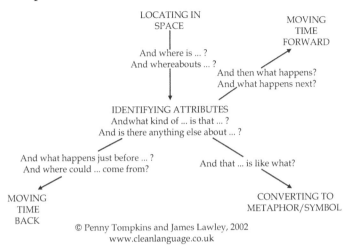

© Penny Tompkins and James Lawley, 2002
www.cleanlanguage.co.uk

nothing, or a simple…and?' (said with a tone of interest and 'tell me more' rather than in an interrogatory tone). Finally, clean language questions are great questions not just for coaching, but for other areas of life or work. At a recent workshop I was running, one of the delegates, a GP, was fascinated by how he could use these questions in his own GP surgery. Equally, in my own business we often get enquiries to run a 'team building session'. My first question is invariably 'And what kind of team building session is that?' Team building in my experience can be anything from bungee jumping to focussing on the team's key objectives for the coming year. Students on my workshops soon appreciate that if, while debriefing an activity, someone states that it was 'interesting' or 'good', my follow up question will always (and I do mean always) be, 'And what kind of interesting is that interesting?'

CLEAN LANGUAGE EXERCISE

Here is a simple way for you and a partner to familiarise yourselves with the most common clean language questions. To start with, both of you need to think about a hobby or pastime you enjoy.

Begin your turn by asking your partner, 'What hobby or pastime do you enjoy?' You then have a couple of minutes to find out more about it, using only four of the clean language questions, namely: '(And) is there anything else about X?', '(And) what kind of X (is that X)?', '(And) where is X?' or '(And) whereabouts is X?' and your partner's own words.

The questions can be asked several times, in any order, about any aspect of what your partner has said. After two or three minutes, swap roles and then share your experiences.

Once you get comfortable with these four questions you can practise including some or all of the remaining five basic clean language questions.

The greatest danger for most of us is not that our aim is too high and we miss it, but that it is too low and we reach it.

Michelangelo

CHAPTER FIVE

GOALS, ISSUES, IDEAS?

IS IT A COACHING GOAL, IDEA OR ISSUE?

A number of years ago I attended the NLP Conference in London. One of the speakers was Shelle Rose Sharvet, author of *Words that Change Minds*, and she started her session with the following story.

'An old man was living in a hotel. One day he went down to reception and said to the receptionist, "Young lady, I have a problem".

The receptionist smiled brightly and replied, "Sir, we have no problems here, only opportunities".

The old man paused, and then replied, "Well I don't know if it's a problem or an opportunity, but there's a woman in my room".'

Rose Sharvet went on to argue that the trigger that makes most people seek a coach is actually not a goal; it is a problem or an issue. What people want to work on in coaching are issues that they want to move away from. They want the coach to help them with these issues.

Rose Sharvet's comments struck a chord with me – and with a lot of the audience. The popular GROW Model (Goal, Reality, Options, Will) is a great coaching model, very effective and easy to use, particularly for novice coaches (and for these reasons we'll be covering it in the next chapter). However, the model does rather assume that coachees turn up for coaching with clear positive goals. My own experience is that, whilst this sometimes happens, more often coachees have 'muddy' goals or ideas or an issue they are wrestling with that they would like to resolve or explore through coaching. I've lost track of the number of times trainee coaches have told me that their experiences of coaching in 'real life' have been quite different to coaching colleagues in the training class. A frequent lament is that their coachee had not really had a goal, more a series of issues, and it had taken the coach the whole of the first session to agree a 'goal' to work on. The coach had become accustomed to their fellow trainee coaches always having a nice positive goal to work with in practice sessions and had assumed that this is how it would be in 'real life'. And of course it isn't.

On a recent coach training programme I was running I had just finished doing a live demonstration of a particular technique and I invited the delegates to get themselves into coaching triads and have a go. I was quite taken aback when one of the delegates said to me, 'It's great having all this free coaching yourself, but I'm starting to run out of issues to work on. I've solved all my problems. I'm going to have to have a good think before it's my turn to be coached.'

I was surprised and immediately responded, 'Well it doesn't have to be an issue, it could be an idea, maybe a sporting challenge.' (I knew he was a keen runner and cyclist). And then I couldn't help myself: 'How about that 10K time of yours…could that be a goal?'

His eyes lit up immediately. 'Great idea! I'm going to work on doing my best ever 10K race next month.'

The delegate went off to work in his chosen coaching triad and I was left reflecting on what exactly is the trigger that makes most people seek a coach. Is it a goal or an idea, or is it more often a problem or an issue?

In summary, I think it can be both and very much depends on whether we are more 'towards' or 'away from' in our thinking. Put another way, where is the energy? Is it more push energy (moving away from) or pull energy (being drawn towards)? To get started on something we often need a trigger, something that we want to get away from – for example 'I don't want to be overweight anymore'. However, to maintain momentum we need to have more towards thinking and be moving towards the thing we want – for example 'I want to be slim and healthy'.

Whether our coachee presents us with an idea (goal, challenge, opportunity) or an issue (problem) one of the first tasks for us as a coach is to help our coachee get this idea or issue into a format they can work with in coaching.

Other important considerations for us as coaches are the limitations that our coachee may already have placed around their idea/issue. I am sure many of you will have come across the popular 'Nine Dots' puzzle illustrated in figure 4 below.

The goal of the puzzle is to link all nine dots using four straight lines or fewer, without lifting the pen and without tracing the same line more than once.

Figure 4 The Nine Dots Puzzle

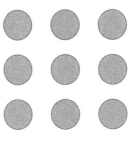

EXAMPLE SOLUTIONS ARE PROVIDED AT THE END OF THIS CHAPTER.

Invariably people struggle to find a solution because, instead of nine dots, they see a square and make an assumption that they cannot draw lines outside of the square, i.e. they did not 'think outside the box'. Other assumptions include that the line has to go through the centre of a dot instead of merely touching each dot As demonstrated in figure 5 at the end of the chapter.

There is a popular story of the elephant in the circus that I often tell on coaching programmes.

One day a young boy went to visit a circus and he saw a huge elephant tied to a small pole with a rope. The elephant just stood there. The young boy thought the elephant looked really miserable and wondered why he didn't use his enormous strength and mass and break away from the stick. Eventually he asked one of the circus men why the elephant did not break free. The man told him that when the elephant was very young he had been tied to the stick in the same way. He didn't like it and tried to escape. But try as he might the rope and pole were too strong for him and eventually the elephant gave up. So now, many years later, the elephant still believed he could not escape from the pole, and remained standing in the same place, despite the fact that he could now easily escape.

I remember relating this story at a workshop I was running on the theme of change a number of years ago. At the coffee break one of the delegates came up to me and said:

'You know that story you told about the elephant, well I have a similar story. A friend of mine rescued a donkey from a donkey sanctuary and gave it a new home in a field with her ponies. This donkey had retired from a life working on Blackpool beach where it used to give donkey rides. My friend thought it would be lovely to let the donkey roam free in the field and play with her ponies, but instead all it did was walk in a straight line for 100 metres, stop, eat some grass and then turn round and walk back. It did that all day long.'

Both stories are, I believe, good illustrations of how we can put limitations on our abilities. Maybe we tried to do something when we were younger and failed and believe we are still unable to do it. Maybe we are so used to doing something a certain way that we believe that is the only way, there is no better way. These limitations are often referred to as limiting beliefs.

'Typical' limiting beliefs that we may hear when we are coaching include:

- 'I must work very long hours to be successful.'
- 'I'm too young.'
- 'I'm too inexperienced.'
- 'I'm in too junior a position in the company.'
- 'No pain – no gain.'
- 'It's not my place to challenge.'
- 'It's not my place to offer a solution.'
- 'I need to be rich to be happy.'
- 'Success takes a long time.'
- 'Most people are luckier than me.'
- 'I can't trust people.'
- 'I never get what I want.'
- 'Other people are better than me.'
- 'I don't deserve to succeed.'
- 'I've reached my limits.'
- 'I can't…'

As coaches, our role is to spot these limiting beliefs or assumptions and challenge them – to encourage our coachee to take a different perspective – to think 'outside the box'. Powerful questions, covered in Chapter Four, are an excellent way of challenging limiting beliefs.

Here are some useful questions that I use in coaching to help my coachee really explore their idea or issue. The questions have their origins in NLP and are often referred to as Well Formed Outcomes. The questions are also useful in helping our coachee step into the future and imagine what success would be like for them. They get to try on their goal and experience exactly what that is like for them.

Question 1. What is it that you really want?

The intention behind this question is to establish real clarity about the coachee's expectations, i.e. what is it they really want? The question is also phrased to encourage the coachee to state their outcome in positive terms, i.e. 'towards' rather than 'away from' thinking. Despite your best efforts you may well find that your coachee has a preference for stating their outcome in away from thinking, in which case a useful follow up question is, 'What would you like instead?'

EXAMPLE:

Coach: *What is it that you really want?*

Coachee: *Not to be stuck in this same job in five years' time.*

Coach: *So, what would you like instead?*

Coachee: *To be in a role that challenges and interests me.*

The coachee is now in a more towards way of thinking and you can continue to explore the specifics of their outcome.

Question 2. So where are you now in relation to your outcome?

This question encourages the coachee to specify the present situation. How close or far off is their outcome? Have they made a start yet? What have they tried that has/hasn't worked? How big a stretch is their outcome?

Question 3. Imagine that you have your outcome now. What would be different? What are you seeing, hearing and feeling? What is important to you about achieving your outcome?

This stage helps the coachee build a strong and compelling image of achieving their outcome. The question engages all of the senses and encourages the coachee to build as rich a picture as possible of what success would be like for them. I often find that this is one of the most powerful questions as it really gets the coachee to associate with their outcome. It becomes truly their outcome. They start to appreciate that their outcome can become their reality. Of course it's a technique that is well practised by sportspeople. Prior to the 100 metres final at the last Olympics every single one of the athletes in the final would know what it would be like to win that race. Exactly what they would be seeing, hearing and feeling – because that is what they have rehearsed time and time again.

Question 4. How will you know you have achieved your goal?

This question encourages your coachee to articulate their evidence criteria. For some outcomes this may be quite straightforward. For example, 'I've completed my first 10K race'. Other outcomes may have more criteria which need to be explored and clarified.

Question 5. Is this goal congruently desirable?

This question invites the coachee to consider their goal afresh. Is it in keeping with who they are? It is quite an unusual question and can be incredibly powerful. Often we carry around goals which are not actually ours. They are things that we feel we should be doing. Perhaps we have even been told that we should be doing them or they are a great opportunity for us. The trouble is they do not really fit with us and who we are. For example, I may have an outcome of being promoted into a sales manager role because I believe that is the natural next step for me and that is the obvious career route in my organisation. The trouble is I love being a sales person. Sales is in my DNA. I'm fantastic at it! I love dealing with customers. I hate internal politics and paperwork, and being in the office bores me. So is being a sales manager in keeping with who I am? Probably not, and I need to do some more serious thinking before committing to that as an outcome for myself. Otherwise I may find that I achieve my outcome and find myself thoroughly miserable in a role I do not enjoy and which does not play to my strengths.

Question 6. Is your outcome self-initiated and self-maintained?

This question encourages the coachee to focus on how much direct control they have over their outcome. Are they able to get started straightaway or do they need help or permission from someone else? Can they maintain momentum themselves or are they going to need support or encouragement from elsewhere? How does their outcome dovetail with what other people want? For example, if my goal is to run a marathon then I am going to have to put in some serious hours of training which will undoubtedly impact on my personal life. This may be an obstacle right from the start. However, if my partner has been talking about taking up running and we could perhaps do some running together as part of my marathon training then maybe that would work for both of us.

Question 7. Is your outcome appropriately contextualised?

This question is about getting your coachee to pause and double check that they have clearly defined the context for their outcome. Where do they want to achieve this outcome? When do they want to achieve it by? And with whom?

Question 8. Is your outcome ecological?

This is certainly a different question, and you may be wondering if this means considering whether your goal is eco-friendly or not. In fact the question is all about highlighting any wider implications of the outcome and any potential 'price to pay' – in which case is the coachee prepared to pay this? This is, I believe, a really useful question, and one which does not appear in most coaching models.

An example I often provide by way of illustration is that I may have a goal of attaining a figure like a super model, but is there a price to pay for my outcome? Well, yes! I'm sure I would have to eat considerably less than I do at present, drink very little alcohol, and going out for meals with friends would be a real treat not a regular occurrence. So, am I prepared to pay that price? Well, no, absolutely not. So I may as well let go of that goal now, rather than continue to hang on to it wistfully, because I'm simply not prepared to pay that price.

There are a range of ecology questions which are provided below. Some of them take a little thinking about to understand what the question is even asking. However, they can be useful questions to ask your coachee to ensure they are focussing on the wider implications of their outcome.

- For what purpose do you want this?
- What will you gain or lose if you have it?
- What will happen when you get it?
- What won't happen when you get it?
- What will happen if you don't get it?
- What won't happen if you don't get it?

Question 9. What resources are needed?

This last question provides a final reality check. What resources are required – time, money, people, etc. The question also encourages the coachee to start thinking about next steps. What can they commit to right now?

A number of years ago I coached Sam. Sam had a senior role in a large multi- national professional services organisation. He did not really have a clear goal, just a general idea that he had been in his current role for two years and it was time to move on to the next challenge. He wanted to stay with the organisation and had recently been approached about a secondment to the States. He was very excited about this opportunity.

I started asking Sam the Well Formed Outcome questions to help him get some clarity around his goal. Sam answered the first questions with ease and enthusiasm. He articulated his outcome very clearly and in the positive. He had no problem imagining success and describing this to me, and, yes, his outcome was definitely congruently desirable for him. Things started to change when we got to question six, 'Is your outcome self-initiated and self-maintained?' Now his outcome started to have a wider implication. He needed to consider his wife and young family and how a move to the States would affect them. When we got to the ecological check there was a definite shift in the energy in the room. I asked 'Is there a price to pay for your outcome?' to which Sam immediately stated that yes, there was. He went on to explain that he had two young children and a third on the way. In his own words, his wife was a real homemaker and was really close to her mother who lived nearby. He couldn't imagine her moving to the States without her support network.

All of a sudden the easy responses, the clear and well-articulated goal, started to evaporate. Sam now seemed far less convinced about his outcome. Yes, his wife knew and had been positive about a potential move to the States, but he had not been too specific about timing and she did not know about this current potential opportunity. We spent the next hour exploring the ecological aspects of

Sam's outcome. There was definitely a price to pay. The question was, was Sam prepared to pay that price?

By the end of the session Sam had a clear way forward mapped out that he felt would work for both himself and his family. He could accept the secondment and he could move to the States for the first month on his own, settle in and find a home for the family. He could then bring his family out there a month later, and he was going to suggest to his wife that her parents came too. Her father had recently retired and he felt they would relish the opportunity of coming with them. At the end of the session he felt comfortable that he had a potential solution that would work for him and would also present a fantastic opportunity for all of the family.

For me it was a powerful example of the ecology check in action. Deep down Sam knew there were some issues, but he was not really facing up to them. Asking 'Is there a price to pay?' made him face up to the issue and decide whether he was prepared to pay the price or not.

FOOD FOR THOUGHT

1. Is your coachee working on a problem, issue, goal, idea? Resist the temptation to start coaching and spend some time clarifying the problem/issue/goal/idea.
2. Be alert for limiting beliefs and challenge them where appropriate.
3. Explore your coachee's goal/issue with them using the well-formed outcome questions so they are clear that this goal/issue is something they want to spend time and energy on.

Figure 5 Some solutions to the nine dot exercise

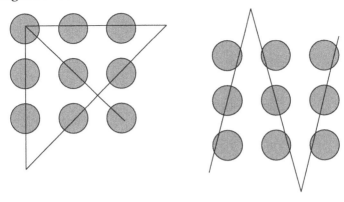

The following are some solutions to the nine dot exercise in figure 4

*'Would you tell me please, which way
I ought to go from here?' said Alice.
'That depends a good deal on where
you want to get to,' said the cat.
'I don't much care where,' said Alice.
'Then it doesn't matter which way you
go,' said the cat.*

**Alice through the looking glass,
Lewis Carroll**

CHAPTER SIX

THE GROW MODEL

I know a number of coaches who claim they don't follow any coaching model when they coach. They follow their instincts, ask questions, listen to the responses and ask the next question they think of, based on the response they have just received. Certainly in my own coaching practice I find that, having started out following frameworks and processes, I tend to work more now with my intuition rather than any particular model. However, I equally know coaches who like the structure of a model, and certainly, when you are just starting out as a coach, trying to remember to ask open questions, use clean language, remember powerful questions, mirror and match body language, allow pauses, etc. can seem too much to remember. I recall, when I first started coaching, really struggling to listen to responses because I was trying to frame my next killer question. So, if you're fairly new to coaching, you might find it useful to start off with a coaching model.

The most well-known coaching model is the GROW Model. If you pick up a book on coaching, you will undoubtedly find a reference to GROW and the various steps of the model. GROW is always the first coaching model that I introduce to students. I've found that the vast majority of people find it simple to use, it has a logical flow to it and, in contrast to other more complex models, it is easy to commit the four stages to memory.

The GROW Model was created by Graham Alexander during the 1980s, based on the work of Tim Gallwey, author of *The Inner Game of Tennis*. It was later brought to prominence by Sir John Whitmore in his book, *Coaching for Performance*. GROW has a strong sports coaching flavour to it, and I find it is straightforward to use in situations where there is a clear goal, and particularly a performance related goal – for example, 'I want to improve my presentation skills'. The stages of GROW focus on the following four areas:

GOAL – WHAT IS THE GOAL?

This stage is about identifying the coaching outcomes: what the coachee wants from the coaching session(s). Here we may work with the coachee to distinguish between the end goal: one which is seldom totally within their control, but which provides their overall motivation, and a performance goal: one which is largely within their control and a means of measuring their progress.

For example, taking a sporting analogy, I may initially present my goal as being to win a particular marathon race next year. Whilst this may be highly inspirational for me as an individual, it certainly isn't totally within my control – I'm sure a number of other athletes in the same race will have the same goal. So, whilst this may be a good end goal for me, it would be useful for me to have some intermediate goals or a performance goal to work on. For example, my performance in other shorter distance races as a build-up or obtaining a personal best.

GROW also employs a technique of testing commitment to the goal to gauge whether the coachee is emotionally as well as intellectually committed. This test is in the form of the question, 'On a scale of 1 to 10, 10 being high and 1 being low, how committed are you to your goal?' If the coachee is less than 10 out of 10, this is a good time to sound out if their goal is really achievable or should it be changed? How will achievement of the goal impact on the coachee? What would make it a 10?

Once the Goal has been fleshed out and agreed, attention is turned to the next stage.

REALITY – WHAT IS THE CURRENT REALITY?

This stage explores the context and background to the goal. Where is the coachee now in relation to their goal? What have they tried so far? What is the gap between their desired outcome and the current situation? What are the issues – the stakeholders, obstacles, resistance, pressure and problems relevant to the journey towards achieving the goal? What forces are working for and against the goal?

This stage continues until the nature of the outcome is fully understood.

OPTIONS – WHAT ARE ALL THE OPTIONS?

When I'm teaching the GROW Model I always tell my delegates at this stage that this is where, as a coach, they really 'earn' their money. As we explored in the previous chapter in the nine dots exercise and the story of the elephant, as humans we are inclined to limit our thinking and stay within our own 'box' of what we know.

As an illustration, just take a moment and look around the room you are sitting in right now and notice everything that is brown. Look closer and harder and see what you notice now that you hadn't spotted before.

Now close your eyes and bring to mind everything that is blue. Did you struggle to do so? You probably did because you had previously directed all your attention on something else, i.e. the colour brown.

A similar pattern follows in coaching. When you ask your coachee what options they have, they will generally offer up one or two off the top of their head. These options will be the ones that they have already been thinking about, that they could imagine doing, that relate most closely to the types of things they have done before. Our job as coach is to open their eyes to other, perhaps slightly different, options – getting them to notice the colour blue instead of just focussing on the brown.

The Options stage is, therefore, about encouraging the coachee to think outside of their usual points of reference and patterns of thinking, challenging the coachee to think laterally and consider all the possibilities before beginning to evaluate them. In this stage 'What if?' questions can be very powerful to break through negative assumptions or limiting beliefs.

Only when all of the options have been identified does the coachee start to evaluate the options and choose the option or options which they believe to be the best.

Once this stage is complete it's time to move into the action phase.

WILL – WHAT WILL YOU DO AND WHEN?

In this stage the coach works with the coachee to develop a plan of action. This will necessitate thinking through all aspects of the planning: who must be informed? Who needs to be involved? What resources are required? What tasks/actions need to be completed and by whom? What milestones should be set?

Finally it's time to test commitment to the plan. The coach asks the coachee to score their newly-created plan on a scale of 1 to 10 to ascertain just how committed they are to it. If the score is less than 7 or 8 then maybe the plan needs revisiting.

For me, the beauty of GROW is that it flows well and has a very clear structure that is easily remembered. Just knowing the stages outlined above, you can easily create your own questions.

If you are just starting out coaching you may find some additional prompt questions useful, and I have therefore included below the questions I use on my coaching programmes. You may notice that I've woven in some of the questions from the Well Formed Outcomes in Chapter Five. I think these additional questions work well with the GROW Model.

You'll probably notice a question in the Options section – 'Would you like another suggestion?' – which may appear contrary to a non-directive approach to coaching and permission to pass on all my wisdom as a coach. However, you'll also notice that this question comes right at the end of the section, when the coachee has exhausted all of their own options, and so you may need to rein in your enthusiasm. Equally the question is deliberately posed as a closed question, and so your coachee could say, 'No, I'm fine, thank you'. Offer up your advice with caution.

There is no requirement to ask all of the questions in a section, but I would recommend that you make sure you have really explored a stage before moving on to the next one.

ACTIVITY – STEPS IN THE GROW MODEL

GOAL

Step 1

What are you looking for from this discussion? (Bearing in mind the time available.)

What do you want to achieve? (E.g. next steps, a short list, a decision.)

Step 2

Is there a long-term goal? If so, what is it?

Is this an end goal or a performance goal?

If it's an end goal, what is a performance goal related to it?

Are there any intermediate goals?

Have you stated your goal in the positive? (If not, what would you like instead?)

How much personal control or influence do you have over your goal?

Is your goal congruently desirable? Is it in keeping with who you are?

How does your goal fit with what other people want?

What will you gain by achieving your goal? What will you lose? Do you still want your goal? What would need to be added to make it personally worthwhile for you?

Imagine you've achieved your goal. What are you seeing/hearing/feeling?

How will you measure success? What is an objective measure? What is a subjective measure?

On a scale of 1 to 10 how committed are you to achieving your goal? (If the score is less than 10, what would make it 10?)

REALITY

Step 3

Where are you now in relation to your goal?

What are the facts now? What is definitely so?

Where are you now out of 10?

What are the reasons for the score?

Step 4

What have you done so far?

What have you done that's worked?

What have you done that hasn't worked?

What effects have any action steps had?

Have you moved forward?

What are the major constraints to finding a way forward?

When things are going badly on this issue, what is the effect on you? (E.g. stress)

What excuses would you give if you didn't achieve your goal? (E.g. time)

Take a moment…Is your goal still relevant and valid? If not, how would you restate your goal?

OPTIONS

Step 5

What could you do to move this forward?

What options do you have?

Who could help?

If you had more time, what could you do?

If you had less time, but still had to move it forward, what could you do?

If you were the CEO what could you do?

What might you do if you knew you couldn't fail?

What quality in you could be enhanced to help you? How could that quality be enhanced?

If you had a magic wand, what would you most like to change, and to what?

If you asked the wisest person you know, what would they say?

What advice would you give to a friend in your position?

What else could you do?

Would you like another suggestion?

Step 6

Take a moment to review your list of options. Weigh up the pros and cons of each option.

Rate each option on a scale of 1 to 10 based on your level of interest in pursuing this option. Include the option of doing nothing at all.

WILL

Step 7

Which option or options are you going to choose? (They can be part of one or more than one.)

When will you do it/them? (Be specific. ASAP is not a diary commitment.)

What is your first step? Are there any quick wins?

Is this on track for the objective of this discussion?

Step 8

What could get in the way?

What obstacles could you face? How will you overcome them?

Step 9

Who needs to know about your plans?

What support do you need? From whom?

How and when are you going to get it?

Step 10

Give yourself a rating on commitment level. This is the likelihood of you carrying out the action. Your commitment to do your bit. Your effort – not your chances of success with the outcome. If your score is less than 10:

- Can you lower your target?
- Can you extend the timescales?

- Can you do part of it? A first step?
- What extra information is needed?
- What are the possible effects – if your commitment is less than 10/10?
- Make it 10.

GROW IN ACTION

I'd just finished introducing the GROW Model during a coaching programme and asked for a volunteer to come to the front with me and do a demo. I was careful to scope my request first – I asked for someone who had something that they wanted to work on for the next twenty minutes; probably not the biggest issue in their life that they were wrestling with right now, but something that they cared about sufficiently and were prepared to invest some personal effort into. Joe immediately volunteered and came to join me at the front.

I started off by reminding Joe that we had about twenty minutes and asked what he'd like to achieve from the session. Joe stated that he wanted to improve his time management skills. I continued to ask questions so that Joe could be really clear about his goal. It turned out that Joe's biggest issue was his email. He currently had a large number of emails in his inbox, and he wanted to get this down to a manageable number and develop some processes for dealing with emails moving forward. What emerged for Joe was an overarching goal with a number of intermediate steps – an immediate one and then some longer term ones. Joe stated that he was completely committed to investing some time and effort into his goal and scored himself a 10.

Having scoped Joe's goal we moved to Reality. Joe currently had in excess of 11,000 emails in his inbox, some read, some unread. Everything came into the one inbox and was all mixed up together. The situation was starting to cause Joe stress – he worried that he sometimes missed important emails and that he simply hadn't read some emails. Also, he was being badgered by the IT department as he was taking up too much space on the server. Joe outlined a few strategies that he had tried so far, including deleting a few emails each day, but to date he'd made very little progress and had coped by ignoring the problem.

Having explored Reality, we moved to Options. As Joe's coach I had some very interesting self-talk going on. I too tend to be a bit of an email hoarder, but I've developed some strategies over the years that work for me, and there was a large part of me that wanted to share my wisdom with Joe. But I kept myself in check.

'So what Options do you have?' I asked.

Joe started to outline some Options: setting himself a target of deleting a few emails each day, creating some folders and assigning the emails to folders, asking IT for more space. He soon dried up.

'So what else could you do?' I asked. Joe sat and thought for a while, and then volunteered that he could identify someone who does manage their emails well and ask them for help, or he could pick a date and delete everything before that date. Slowly he added a few more options. Finally there were no more options.

'Would you like another suggestion?' I enquired. Joe nodded enthusiastically. 'Well, something that worked for me was to set up some simple filtering folders, for example one for anything that I'm only copied into, one for any newsletters that I subscribe to which are nice to read if I have time, etc.'

'Great idea,' said Joe and added this option to his list. By now Joe had a fairly long list of options, and I asked him to review them and weigh up the pros and cons of each. He went through each one and scored them from 1 to 10 based on his level of interest in pursuing this option. Some immediately emerged as non-starters – for example, he'd already tried the delete so many emails a day approach and that hadn't worked for him.

As he went through this process, a couple of options emerged as favourites – doing a dramatic intervention to cull a good number of emails, and then taking time to set up some folders going forward. Joe decided to go with both of these. We explored the obstacles to the former in some detail. Was that simply too risky? Reckless even? At first Joe thought it was, but then he realised that actually most emails he really had to read and action tended to come from specific sources, and if he didn't respond within a timeframe to an urgent email, he was always sent a chaser, and so what had seemed a huge risk was, he felt, manageable. He set himself a specific date, one week later, by which time he committed to doing his final filter before deleting any surplus emails. He also committed to booking some time with a colleague to get some advice on setting up folders and filters. We explored what obstacles he might face, and, on reflection, Joe felt that one week was perhaps too tight and moved the deadline back a further week. We ended the session with Joe declaring his commitment level as 10/10.

One month later the group reconvened for the next module of the programme. Everyone was keen to hear how Joe had got on. We didn't have to wait long. Joe shared how he'd taken time on the Sunday after the workshop to go through his emails and rescue any important ones. On the following day he'd deleted thousands of emails, most of which he'd come to realise were just clutter. Completing this task had, he shared, been both scary and liberating, but one month on he hadn't missed, or been chased on, anything that he had deleted. He had also set up some email filtering systems for himself and was finally starting to feel on top of his emails.

Six months later we reached the end of the programme. Joe shared how it had been a huge 'aha' moment for himself when he had first realised the power of coaching. He still hadn't missed any of his deleted emails and had continued his 'new' way of working.

As mentioned at the start of this chapter, the GROW Model works best with performance-related goals, when it is possible to create a specific tangible goal that can be measured. It tends to work less well with more 'fuzzy' outcomes – for example, when a coachee doesn't really know what they want, other than it's not what they've got now, and/or coaching has been suggested to someone as a means of developing their leadership style or their relationships with others. Or perhaps they have received feedback, for example via a multi-rater or 360° feedback survey that they don't really understand. In the latter situation it's probably more useful to explore blind spots and heightening self-awareness with your coachee rather than slavishly trying to get your coachee to think about a goal which is Specific, Measurable, Achievable, Relevant and Time-bound (SMART). On other occasions your coachee may turn up for a session with something that's troubling them or that they just want to reflect upon – maybe preparing for a specific meeting next week or using the coaching space to explore some new strategies.

In such instances a model such as GROW may not be appropriate, and some of the tools, techniques and ways of exploring situations in a different way outlined in the following chapters may be more helpful.

The still point of the turning world

Burnt Norton,
T.S. Eliot

CHAPTER SEVEN

WORK-LIFE BALANCE/ CAREER TRANSITIONS

Sometimes coachees turn up for coaching not really knowing what they want. They feel a bit 'stuck'. They don't want to be in this job much longer, they are feeling stale, but they are not sure what to do next. Perhaps they are thinking of taking the plunge and leaving corporate life to do something on their own, but are not quite convinced that it is the right thing to do or whether the timing is right. Maybe their role is changing or has changed and they have been told it is time for them to move on. Maybe their role has now got so big and all-encompassing that they feel work has taken over and they have no life beyond work. Or they may have recently changed roles and are struggling to come to terms with the responsibilities and demands of this new role. As a coach I refer to this space as working with work-life balance or career transitions.

Questions I often ask coachees when they are feeling stuck are:

- 'What do you look forward to when:
- you get up in the morning?
- you go home at night?'

The answers to the above questions can be quite illuminating for the coachee. How much sense of achievement and enjoyment are they getting from their job? How much stimulation do they get from social interactions with colleagues?

Clutterbuck (2003) defines work-life balance as:

A state where an individual manages real or potential conflict between different demands on his or her time and energy in a way that satisfies their needs for well-being and self-fulfilment.

He identifies two distinct forms of 'stretch':

- Positive stretch – tasks where you are challenged intellectually and/or physically. Positive stretch can also be negative if the gap between current capability and the demands of the task is too great.
- Negative stretch – where the work does not involve any learning, but the volume is beyond your capacity to cope.

All of this, I believe, raises some interesting questions and suggests that work-life balance is a very personal equation. What for you may be perfect work-life balance might for me be a total nightmare. It's really about understanding what we want to achieve in different parts of our life. Therefore, for me coaching in this space is all about raising self-awareness, helping people move from a space of feeling 'stuck' and not really sure what they want to a space where they are starting to get a sense of what they want to do or what needs to happen. I have a number of tools that I use to help coachees explore issues and gain some more clarity. The layout of this chapter is therefore a little different to the rest and comprises of five tools that I often use when coaching in this space.

TOOL 1 - COACHING WHEELS

Wheels are an excellent way of helping a coachee explore which parts of their life are going well and which parts need some attention. I regularly use wheels in my coaching practice, often sending them to coachees with the invitation to complete them and bring them along to the next session. The nice thing about wheels is that they are very flexible. There is no right or wrong way to complete them, and whatever the coachee does will make sense to them. They are also very visual. My coachee can see that, if this were a real wheel, it would be an incredibly bumpy ride. They don't need me to point this out.

The wheels I use most often are the Wheel of Life and the Wheel of Work.

THE WHEEL OF LIFE EXERCISE

The Wheel of Life is demonstrated in figure 6. For ease I have added labels to the various spokes, but I always stress to my coachees that they can change these labels and use ones which are meaningful to them.

DIRECTIONS

Each section of the wheel has a scale of 0-10, with 0 at the centre representing total dissatisfaction, and 10 at the outside representing total satisfaction. The task is to shade in the segments of each section to the degree to which you are satisfied with that aspect of your life.

You may not spend much time or energy on a certain section, and that may be fine, in which case you are totally satisfied with that area and would shade it all in. Conversely, you may be spending too much of your time in one area, but be very dissatisfied, in which case you would only shade in a small portion of that section.

Figure 6. The Wheel of Life

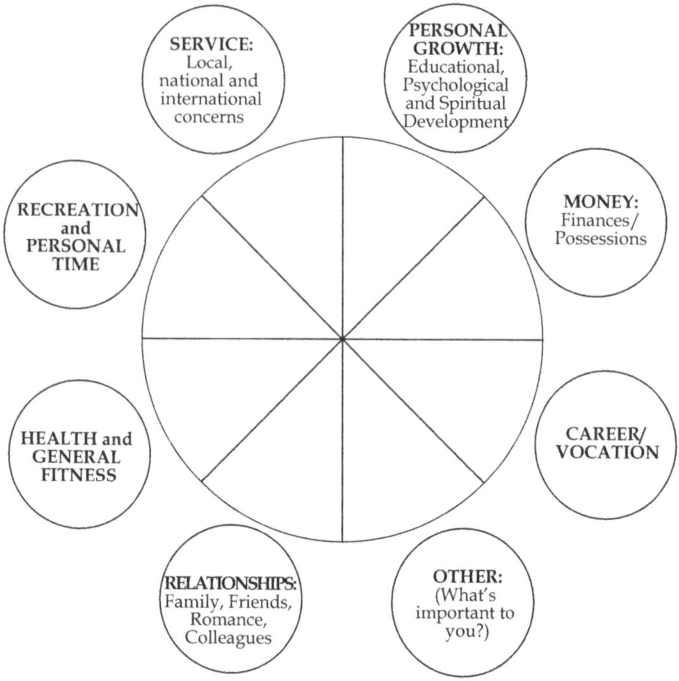

Imagine the new perimeter of the circle represents your Wheel of Life. How smooth is the ride?

THE WHEEL OF WORK EXERCISE

The Wheel of Work is identical to the Wheel of Life, except that the labels on it relate much more to work situations. The labels I use are:

- Personal development: Educational/Professional
- Money: Financial Reward/Earnings
- Career Progress
- Purpose and Passion: What's Important to You?
- Work Relationships: Colleagues/Bosses/Team Members
- Recognition and Support

- Work/Life Balance
- Work: Content and Process

The directions are exactly the same as for the Wheel of Life.

When using the above wheels I will typically email them to my coachee, or hand them out at the end of a coaching session, and invite my coachee to complete one or both wheels and bring them along to our next session. At the next session my approach is always a light touch.

- 'Did you complete them?'
- 'How did you get on?'
- 'Which one did you complete?'
- If they completed both: 'Which one did you find easier/harder?'

I then pretty much hand over to the coachee and ask them to explain their wheel(s) to me.

Over the years I have seen many different ways of completing the wheels, and so my approach is very much just to listen as my coachee tells me the story of their wheel(s). When they have finished, I will ask a few open questions, for example:

- 'What did you get from this activity?'
- 'Which areas of your wheel do you feel need some attention?'

The coachee may identify a number of areas of their wheel(s) that they want to work on during our coaching time together, or they may just identify one for us to work on during that particular session. I tend to go with the energy of the coachee.

A short action-focused way of coaching using the wheels is now described.

COACHING ACTIVITY USING THE WHEEL OF LIFE OR WHEEL OF WORK

Invite your coachee to select an area to work on. Useful questions are:

- 'What is your goal/outcome with regards to creating a better Work-Life Balance?'

OR

- 'What part of your wheel would you like to change?'

Once they have articulated their outcome for the session, invite your coachee to:

- 'List out loud, in no particular order, all of the things that you believe are blockages and are stopping you from getting what you really want in this area.'

Make a note of the list as your coachee speaks it aloud. You may need to keep asking your coachee to repeat/summarise information so that you can note their list accurately. Where appropriate you may simply need to ask your coachee:

- 'How would you summarise that?'

OR

- 'How would you like me to capture that for you?'

Once they have exhausted their list, go through the list of blockages together and ask your coachee to identify which items they believe to be certain known facts and which are in fact assumptions they are making.

For example, your coachee may have identified 'I am not qualified' or 'My manager wouldn't let me' as blockages. Are these known facts or are they actually at this point assumptions?

Work through each item together. Even when items are identified as 'facts' you may still want to explore, if appropriate, why that fact is blocking your coachee.

Once you have gone through the list and categorised each item, encourage your coachee to think about options for removing blockages. Always allow your coachee to come up with what options he/she could choose to remove the blockage first, and only then offer your own ideas. Only do the latter if your coachee agrees that they would find your suggestions useful.

Finally, invite your coachee to write down all the possible action points that they intend to take forward from the exercise, including when they will carry them out.

TOOL 2 – WHAT HAVE I ACHIEVED?

The 'What have I achieved?' tool is a variant of the Wheels of Life and Work. I often email it to coachees with the wheels and suggest that they may want to complete it. The activity is very straightforward. Coachees are asked to consider the statement:

'I am 85 looking back on my life and I am pleased. This is a record of what I have achieved:'

And then list their achievements against the following criteria:

- Career
- Hobbies/interests
- Family and friends
- Other

Some prefer the wheels and leave this activity untouched. Others complete it in great detail, and volunteer that it gave them clarity about what they have achieved so far, what they still want to achieve and how long they potentially have to achieve this. For some, this is ages – 'I'm only twenty-four so there is really no rush'. For others

125

there is more of a sense of 'Well I need to get cracking, I'm now fifty-five and I haven't even started on this.'

TOOL 3 – WHAT ARE YOUR VALUES? COACHING ACTIVITY

This next tool is useful for exploring with your coachee what is important to them about their job or career. Often referred to as a values elicitation exercise, the exercise helps uncover our 'values'.

If you look up 'value' in the dictionary you will find it is classified as a noun with a wide range of meanings, including monetary or material worth, the relative duration of a tone or rest in music, an assigned or calculated numerical quantity, or a principle, standard or quality considered worthwhile or desirable.

'Value' in the context of this activity is used to describe those things that are important to us and driving our actions. More explicitly, values are defined as a deep unconscious belief system about what is important and what is good or bad for us. The activity is described below.

VALUES ELICITATION EXERCISE

STEP 1: STANDARD ELICITATION

As a coach, work with your coachee to define what is important to them, e.g. 'career', 'work'. Once you have identified this, follow the next steps:

- Ask 'What is important to you about... (your career)?' If the word/value they give you is of too low a level or is a

126

behaviour (e.g. 'Having a tidy desk'), ask: 'What is important about that?' or 'What is this an example of?' or 'X for what purpose?'

- Write down the values for your coachee in their words (encourage them to use one or two words).
- To uncover other values, you can ask: 'What does (each/ this) value mean to you?' and/or 'What has to happen for you to feel this value is fulfilled?'
- Keep going until you get the 'second wave' or your coachee starts to repeat themselves.
- Write down exactly what your coachee says.
- Once your coachee has completed their list, share this with them.

Ask them:

- 'If you had all of this (i.e. these values) in a career/job, would you want it or is anything missing?'
- Write down any additional values.

STEP 2: RANKING THE VALUES

Now ask your coachee: 'Of these values, which is the most important to you?' Write this down first.

Once you have the first value, say 'Assuming you have x, what is the next most important?'

Continue asking this question and writing down the responses until you have the top five or eight.

Rewrite the list of values according to their importance.

NB: Your coachee may find it more useful to rank the values as A/B/C, where 'A' is absolutely essential, 'B' is really nice to have but not essential, and 'C' is 'the icing on the cake'.

STEP 3: TEST

Offer your coachee two jobs, the first with values of 5–8 (or Bs and Cs) and the second with values of 1–4 (or As). Ask them which they would choose. If they choose the one with the higher value, suggest that they revisit their rankings.

Also offer your coachee a job with the values in the ranked order and ask if they would want it. E.g. 'If you had a job with value 1, value 2, etc. up to value 5 (or one with all the As), would you want it?' If the answer is not a congruent yes, ask if there is any other value they would like to add to the list.

STEP 4: REFLECTION

Ask your coachee for their reflections on the activity.

- What is interesting/surprising?
- How well is their current career/work aligned to their values?
- What other insights do they have?
- What are they taking away from the activity?

The above exercise can assist a coachee in uncovering for themselves what is really important for them, particularly if they are at a stage where they need to make some big decisions about their work/career.

Many years ago I was working with Elizabeth. Elizabeth had come to me for coaching as she was feeling very stuck in her job. She was not enjoying the type of work she was doing and didn't find it stimulating. At the time, she was weighing up a number of options and had actually been offered a role in another organisation. When she described the role, she sounded excited and energised, whereas she sounded the complete opposite when she described her current role. I couldn't understand what was preventing her taking the new role. After a time I suggested doing the values elicitation exercise.

Part way through the exercise it started to make sense. Elizabeth's number one value was financial security. There had been a time in her life when she had been the sole provider for her family and it was of paramount importance to her always to be able to do so. 'Stimulating and interesting work' was much lower down the list.

I tested this ranking with Elizabeth. 'So would you continue in a job you found unstimulating and uninteresting but that provided a perceived high level of financial security in favour of a role which was stimulating and interesting but offered a low level of financial security'?

'Yes, definitely' was the unequivocal response. I was momentarily taken aback. I wouldn't make the same choice, but of course I wasn't Elizabeth. The activity provided Elizabeth with clarity about what was really important to her. Ultimately she stayed in her current role for quite some time before she decided conditions were right for her to move on. However, she did so knowing that this was the right thing for her to do.

TOOL 4 - 'WHAT DO I DO BEST?' INVENTORY

This tool is a simple set of questions. These questions form an 'inventory' of what the coachee does best. I usually email these to a coachee inviting them to find some quality time to complete them and bring them back to their next coaching session. The questions I use are as follows:

- What part of my work do I most enjoy?
- What aspect of my work gives me the greatest sense of accomplishment?

129

- What aspect of my work am I best at?
- What was I doing when I was having the most fun with my work?
- What type of people am I most comfortable with?
- How would I describe the values of these people?
- What part of my work brings me the greatest sense of joy and accomplishment?

TOOL 5 – CAREER ANCHORS

I quite frequently coach people who are at a crossroads in their career and not sure about which road they should take. Maybe they have been a technical specialist for a long time and are wondering whether they should move into a commercial or management role. Perhaps they are wondering if now is the time to leave corporate life and venture out on their own. Maybe they are tired of working long hours and wondering if it is time to take life a little easier and perhaps get a less demanding role and/or work fewer hours. When I am doing this kind of crossroads coaching I often suggest that the coachee takes the Career Anchors Inventory (*www.careeranchorsonline. com*). Developed by Edgar Schein, the purpose of this inventory is to stimulate your thoughts about your own areas of competence, your motives and your values. A career anchor is defined by Schein as the one element about your wishes for a job that you would not give up if you were forced to make a choice. It may not reflect what you are doing now, and will often remain stable throughout your career. The questionnaire can be completed online. Whilst the questionnaire alone will not reveal your coachee's career anchor because it is too easy to bias the answers, it will activate their thinking and prepare them for a coaching conversation with you.

IDENTIFYING YOUR CAREER ANCHOR

The following summaries describe the eight career anchors.

TECHNICAL/FUNCTIONAL COMPETENCE

If your career anchor is competence in some technical or functional area, what you would not give up is the opportunity to apply your skills in that area and to continue to develop those skills to an ever-higher level. You derive your sense of identity from the exercise of your skills and are most happy when your work permits you to be challenged in those areas. You may be willing to manage others in your technical or functional area, but you are not interested in management for its own sake and would avoid general management because you would have to leave your own area of expertise.

GENERAL MANAGERIAL COMPETENCE

If your career anchor is general managerial competence, what you would not give up is the opportunity to climb to a level high enough in an organisation to enable you to integrate the efforts of others across functions and to be responsible for the output of a particular unit of the organisation. You want to be responsible and accountable for total results and you identify your own work with the success of the organisation for which you work. If you are presently in a technical or functional area, you view that as a necessary learning experience; however, your ambition is to get to a generalist job as soon as possible. Being at a high managerial level in a function does not interest you.

AUTONOMY/INDEPENDENCE

If your career anchor is autonomy/independence, what you would not give up is the opportunity to define your own work in your own way. If you are in an organisation, you want to remain in jobs that allow you flexibility regarding when and how to work. If you cannot tolerate organisational rules and restrictions to any degree, you seek occupations in which you will have the freedom you seek, such as teaching or consulting. You refuse opportunities for promotion or advancement in order to retain autonomy. You may even seek to have a business of your own in order to achieve a sense of autonomy; however, this motive is not the same as the entrepreneurial creativity described later.

SECURITY/STABILITY

If your career anchor is security/stability, what you would not give up is employment security or tenure in a job or organisation. Your main concern is to achieve a sense of having succeeded so that you can relax. This anchor shows up in concern for financial security (such as pension and retirement plans) or employment security. Such stability may involve trading your loyalty and willingness to do whatever the employer wants from you for some promise of job tenure. You are less concerned with the content of your work and the rank you achieve in the organisation, although you may achieve a high level if your talents permit. As with autonomy, everyone has certain needs for security and stability, especially at times when financial burdens may be heavy or when one is facing retirement. People anchored in this way, however, are always concerned with these issues and build their entire self-images around the management of security and stability.

ENTREPRENEURIAL CREATIVITY

If your career anchor is entrepreneurial creativity, what you would not give up is the opportunity to create an organisation or enterprise of your own, built on your own abilities and your willingness to take risks and to overcome obstacles. You want to prove to the world that you can create an enterprise that is the result of your own effort. You may be working for others in an organisation while you are learning and assessing future opportunities, but you will go out on your own as soon as you feel you can manage it. You want your enterprise to be financially successful as proof of your abilities.

SERVICE/DEDICATION TO A CAUSE

If your career anchor is service/dedication to a cause, what you would not give up is the opportunity to pursue work that achieves something of value, such as making the world a better place to live, solving environmental problems, improving harmony among people, helping others, improving people's safety, curing diseases through new products, and so on. You pursue such opportunities even if it means changing organisations, and you do not accept transfers or promotions that would take you out of work that fulfils your values.

PURE CHALLENGE

If your career anchor is pure challenge, what you would not give up is the opportunity to work on solutions to seemingly unsolvable problems, to win out over tough opponents, or to overcome difficult obstacles. For you, the only meaningful reason for pursuing a job or career is that it permits you to win over the impossible. Some people find such pure challenge in intellectual kinds of work, such as the engineer who is interested only in impossibly difficult designs; some find the challenge in complex multifaceted situations, such as the strategy consultant who is interested only in clients who are about to go bankrupt and have exhausted all other resources; some find it in interpersonal competition, such as the professional athlete or the salesperson who defines every sale as either a win or a loss. Novelty, variety and difficulty become ends in themselves, and if something is easy, it becomes immediately boring.

LIFESTYLE

If your career anchor is lifestyle, what you would not give up is a situation that permits you to balance and integrate your personal needs, your family needs and the requirements of your career. You want to make all of the major sectors of your life work together towards an integrated whole, and you therefore need a career situation that provides enough flexibility to achieve such integration. You may have to sacrifice some aspects of your career (for example, a geographical move that would be a promotion, but would upset your total life situation), and you define success in terms broader than just career success. You feel that your identity is more tied up with how you live your total life, where you live, how you deal with your family situation and how you develop yourself than with any particular job or organisation.

Once my coachee has completed and scored their inventory we use these results as a starting point for a discussion. Are there any surprises in their results? If so what may be the reasons for these? What themes/ messages emerge?

In some respects this activity is similar to the previous values elicitation exercise. The key difference is that the anchors are pre-defined instead of the coachee having to come up with them. The inventory is also a questionnaire, with questions, scores and a profile which some coachees prefer. I therefore tend to use one or the other, depending on who the coachee is and their own preferences around learning. The inventory is very useful in helping the coachee uncover what it is that really drives and motivates them – as opposed to what they feel they should be doing now at this stage in their career.

David was an accountant and had come to me for coaching as he wasn't sure about the direction in which his career was going and whether or not he wanted to make a career move. Towards the end of the second session he mentioned that he had thought about setting up his own business.

'A bit like you have,' he said. 'It'd be great just to be answerable to me, to do something different.'

I briefly described the Career Anchors Inventory and suggested he completed this. David had recently completed the Myers Briggs Type Indicator (MBTI) and I knew that he liked questionnaires and inventories and a structured way of getting feedback and information. David duly went away and completed the questionnaire and returned for our third session. We scored up his completed questionnaire at the session. David's two strongest anchors emerged as Security/Stability and Lifestyle. I knew from my own experience that it would be a real challenge for David to have either of these if he set up his own business. However, I kept my thoughts to myself and asked him lots of clean questions.

David absolutely recognised his profile. He explained that he had been with his company for a good number of years, he still had a final salary pension scheme, and being able to provide for his family was of paramount importance. Equally, whilst he worked hard, he was very careful about not working what he perceived as excessive hours. We then explored to what extent these anchors would be met if he set up his own business. David immediately volunteered that it was extremely unlikely that they would be, and on this basis dismissed this as an option. Instead we spent the rest of our sessions focussing on a) how could he expand/develop his current role to make it more interesting and high profile? And b) what other options were there internally for him to make a lateral career move?

If he hadn't completed Careers Anchors, David may have still reached the same conclusion, but I'm certain it would have taken him a lot longer. The questionnaire helped him get clarity and close off an option which had been exercising a fair amount of time and energy, and instead pursue other options which were a better fit for him.

*Some men see things
as they are and say,
'Why?' I dream of things
that never were and say,
'Why not?'*

George Bernard Shaw

CHAPTER EIGHT

COACHING THROUGH CHANGE

People come to coaching for lots of different reasons, but the bottom line is change. They no longer want things to stay the same and they see that coaching can make that happen. (Whitmore, 2002, p.27).

As discussed in Chapter One, definitions of coaching tend to fall into two different camps: learning and development linked to performance improvement, or coaching to facilitate personal growth and change. My own experience is that the most effective and sustainable coaching involves some element of change. This change can be quite dramatic – for example, the coachee decides on an alternative career choice or way of living their life as part of the process. Other changes may outwardly appear less dramatic, but may still involve significant changes in beliefs, attitudes and behaviour. One former coachee provided the following powerful analogy when reflecting on how coaching had changed him.

I think...this might feel quite strange...but I feel the way I felt after I got married. I remember this very clearly, and I remember talking to my wife about it a day or two after. We'd been going out together for years and lived together at various times, and I didn't feel any different about my relationship with her other than the fact that it felt as if it had an extra couple of layers of foundations in there. There was a very low level emotional stable strength, but there was something else...it had added in the bass notes, or however you want to phrase it, but nothing else felt changed. And it feels a bit like that with coaching. There is nothing fundamentally different, maybe slightly better tuning in places, but there's more depth to foundations if you like, and even a few more hooks to go and hang these on. Whereas if I look at some of the other training, e.g. the MBA, that completely changed the way I think about businesses and I cannot believe that I ever thought about them in any other way than how I think about them now as a result of the MBA. Coaching wasn't as fact-based or as swinging a change as that. It added more depth...the foundation stones. And therefore it is sustained.

In addition, in recent years many of my coaching clients have been wrestling with issues involving enforced change. Their organisation has had a reorganisation and their job has changed or disappeared. Many of my public sector coachees work for organisations that, owing to public sector funding reductions, have been 'forced' into mergers or partnerships with other organisations. The leader who once had a small team of people, all long-standing employees whom they knew really well, now finds that they have inherited another team of people located in a different organisation who they hardly know at all. Their job now is to make this team one team, whilst also wrestling with the challenges of their own, now bigger, role and what exactly this means. All these changes require different ways of thinking, different ways of working and a major rebuilding of the team.

Whilst change can evoke a wide range of emotions in us, research has consistently shown that, as human beings, we tend to respond to enforced change in quite a consistent way. The variable factors are how quickly we will move through any change process and the intensity of the negative emotions that we may experience. The well-known transition curve describes typical responses to enforced change.

THE TRANSITION CURVE HAS FOUR KEY STAGES.

Stage one – Immobilisation/Denial. This stage is characterised by disbelief or resistance. There's often a sense that the change represents the latest *program du jour* which will inevitably give way to the next management fad. Business as usual often predominates. In many respects this is the easiest coping mechanism to adopt: a sense of putting one's head in the sand and ignoring it. As such, it can be the hardest to overcome, and nothing will typically change unless there is some powerful intervention.

Stage two – The Stage of Emotion. This stage is characterised by high levels of energy being consumed in complaining and blaming. In time, anxiety and anger may give rise to despondency, despair and depression. In an organisation, sickness and absenteeism often increase at this stage and key people may choose to leave.

Stage three – Beginning to Turn the Corner. This stage is characterised by people beginning to show an interest by asking questions. 'How will this work?', 'How will my job change?', 'How can I help to implement the change?' There's a high level of energy being expended, but questions still outweigh concrete answers.

Stage four – The Change is Institutionalised. This stage is characterised by people 'walking the talk', feeling and acting empowered. Energy is now being channelled into constructive activities, e.g. problem solving. There may be the belief that 'we've done it', and as a result some momentum may be lost. Complacency may even creep in.

The My Response to Change Model is one I designed based on the transition curve, and is intended to be used as a simple but powerful diagnostic and exploration tool during a coaching conversation with anyone who is facing an uncomfortable situation involving the need to deal with enforced changes in their life.

The model has four quadrants. Each of the quadrants represents a different mindset based on the individual's emotional well-being, self-esteem and morale, i.e. how positive they are feeling about themselves and the perceived amount of control they have in a given situation and the degree to which someone has turned

Figure 7 My Response to Change Model

Disbelief Business as usual **Denial and Resistance**	Walking the talk Feeling and acting empowered Danger of complacency ..... **Acceptance**
Angry Anxious Helpless **Complaining and Blaming**	Showing interest Asking questions .... How... ? **Exploring**

Vertical axis: − Emotional Well-being / Self-Esteem / Morale +

Horizontal axis: Low — Turning the Corner — High

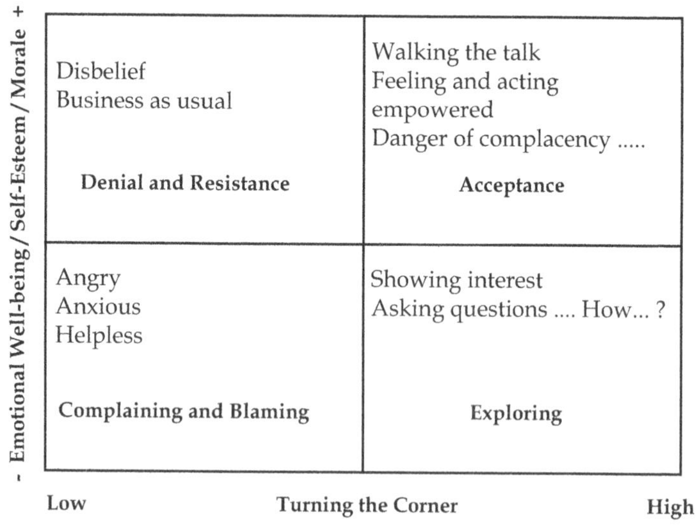

the corner and is starting to explore and even accept the change.

The model helps the coach and coachee explore the coachee's mindset when they are faced with an enforced change. It also helps the coachee explore how they can move from a position of disempowerment to one of empowerment, i.e. how can they turn the corner?

The aim of the model is to help and support the coachee to move as quickly as reasonably possible into the 'Exploring' quadrant and ultimately the 'Acceptance' quadrant. The focus is on the coachee empowering themselves, taking responsibility and action.

I typically have a copy of the model which I place on the table in front of me and my coachee and we explore it together. I listen to the language my coachee is using. Do I hear them being resentful and complaining about the change processes going on? Do they sound angry, as if things are happening to them? Do they sound as if they've given up and they're feeling disempowered? I may reflect back some of my coachee's language, for example, 'What I've heard you say several times is...which quadrant do you think these words belong to?' Recognising where someone is in the change process is the first step. Deciding to do something about it is the next stage.

Some useful coaching questions include:

- Which quadrant do you think you're in at this moment in time?
- In which of the quadrants do you think you are currently living? How long have you been in this quadrant?
- How might you move to the next quadrant?

- What could you be doing to make a start?
- What options do you have for overcoming the blockages to moving on?
- What are other organisations/individuals doing? (A useful question for challenging denial).
- What would be the implications of doing nothing/staying where you are?
- Who do you think could help you?
- What have you tried so far?
- What would be a realistic goal for you?
- What successes have you had so far?
- Now you have achieved x, what is your next goal? (A useful question for challenging complacency).

Movement between quadrants may, of course, only happen slowly. The key is to help the coachee determine their position in the model and then start to explore how they might begin to move forward.

NEUROLOGICAL LEVELS OF CHANGE

Another model I use when working with coaching clients whose outcomes relate to either enforced change or a change which they are personally driving is the Neurological Levels of Change Model.

The concept of neurological levels of change was initially explored by Gregory Bateson, based on the work of Russell and Whitehead in mathematics. Robert Dilts then went on to apply Bateson's concept.

Neurological levels refer to a fundamental hierarchy of organisation in which each level is progressively more encompassing and has a greater psychological impact.

Changing something at a low level is likely to have no, or an insignificant, impact on higher levels. However, changing something at a high level will have a ripple down effect, influencing all lower levels.

I have illustrated how the levels relate to one another, and some of the key questions for each level, in figure 8 below.

Figure 8 Neurological levels of change

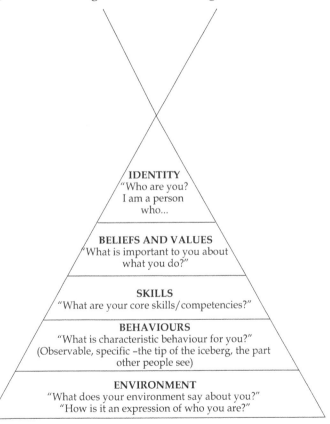

IDENTITY
"Who are you?
I am a person
who...

BELIEFS AND VALUES
"What is important to you about
what you do?"

SKILLS
"What are your core skills/competencies?"

BEHAVIOURS
"What is characteristic behaviour for you?"
(Observable, specific –the tip of the iceberg, the part
other people see)

ENVIRONMENT
"What does your environment say about you?"
"How is it an expression of who you are?"

The model provides a useful appreciation of why a lot of training and development initiatives fail to stick: either because the recipients felt the initiative was a waste of time in the first place or they simply had not really bought into the process. For example, if I go on a presentation skills course, it doesn't matter how much time I spend on putting my message together and crafting superb PowerPoint slides if I fundamentally do not challenge my belief that I am no good at presenting. If I return to work with the same underlying belief, chances are, when I go to do that important presentation next Monday, my performance will not have improved that much as my old doubts, fears and negative self-talk will probably take over and sabotage my performance.

Likewise change can often be introduced in an organisation at a superficial level. Consider two teams, team A and team B. The two teams were recently merged into one team, working to one manager. Currently the teams work in different buildings, and the manager sees this as causing some friction and preventing the teams now working together as one team. However, he tells me it will all be better on Monday when both teams are moving into the same area and will then be co-located in the same building. I smile to myself. Referring back to the Neurological Levels of Change Model, this is, of course, simply an environmental change. Yes, co-locating may contribute to a general sense of 'one team', but, I would argue, it is far more likely to highlight key differences in behaviour, skills, beliefs and identity between the two teams. A fundamental belief that what I do, as a Team A person, is far more skilled and important that what you do, as a Team B person, will continue to reinforce the sense of there being two teams. As the manager of the new team, I need to do a lot of work with the team to create a fresh identity; new beliefs and values for this new team; assess what combined skills we have and whether we need to do some cross-skilling; work with the team to create some agreed ways of working; and help the team create a new team environment, perhaps avoiding the situation where all of Team A sit together and Team B sit together.

The model can therefore be used very effectively in team coaching to enable team members to appreciate at which level they need to make an intervention in order to bring about necessary change. However, I mainly use the model with individual coaching clients, as illustrated in the following example:

It was my second coaching session with Tom. At the first session we had spent a long time discussing his coaching outcomes. Tom had recently been promoted, and had now joined the Executive Team. However, he was struggling to contribute in meetings. He invariably left these meetings wishing he had spoken up or frustrated that he had been thinking something and that someone else had stepped in and made that point. Without explaining the model to him, I asked him to think back to a recent meeting he had attended, and I then asked him some questions and wrote down his responses.

I asked Tom to describe the meeting room and who was sitting where. He described it as offsite, a typical conference room in a hotel. He was there at the start, interacting with the Board members. In the meeting he was sitting at the front by the screen near the Chief Exec, helping him with his presentation. (Environment)

Next I asked Tom to describe his 'typical behaviour' in the meeting: what others would see him doing and saying. He described how he would be asking questions, for example, 'Did you get the pack?' building rapport by discussing sport or technology with the non-Execs. During the meeting he would be taking lots of notes. He would also be facilitating discussions, building consensus and pre-empting questions. (Behaviour)

I then asked Tom to describe his core skills. He said these were facilitating skills, encouraging dialogue, analytical and reasoning skills and interpreting data. He continued that he could make useful interjections, but he 'needed an in', and he was good at using 'Pull' influencing strategies and bringing others in. (Skills)

I asked Tom what was important to him and what he believed about himself. He stated that he believed the Executive Team had a shared passion for what they were trying to achieve as an organisation, that they had an exciting future with buy-in 'to be the best we can be' and that he had been appointed into his new role to make this happen.

Finally I asked Tom to complete the following sentence: 'I am a person who…' to which he stated, 'believes in what we are trying to achieve as an organisation, believes we have genuine choices, has more time to spend on external factors (versus other members of the Board), is younger and more au fait technically'.

I then described the model to Tom, and as I did so, he immediately started to comment on some of the things that he appreciated he was doing which were detracting from the impact he really wanted to create in his new role.

I invited Tom to step into the identity of 'I am the Marketing Director' and imagine himself attending the next Executive Team meeting in a month's time. Holding on to this identity, we revisited each of the levels, starting at the top this time.

Identity. Tom expressed his identity as 'I am the Marketing Director', emphasising the words with real conviction.

Beliefs. This time Tom declared 'I genuinely bring an external perspective, different ways of looking at the situation. I'm passionate about how we achieve what we do, giving our people something to believe in.'

Skills. Tom described his core skills as 'Same as before, plus I'm now using more 'Push' in my influencing style. I have insight and opinion and I own it. I bring insights from having worked for some of the most successful businesses in the UK.'

Behaviour. When he reached this level, Tom remarked that he was now spending his time actively listening and using non-verbal communication and was making very few notes, just the salient points.

Environment. Finally we returned to the environment, and this time I noticed a big difference in Tom and his energy. He commented that he was now sitting at the table with the others. He was within eye range of the Chief Executive. He was using the coffee breaks to interact with the Board.

The exercise was enlightening for Tom. He appreciated that truly stepping into the role, acting as if it was really his by right, immediately brought out some key changes, particularly with regard to the behaviours he exhibited in the meeting and how he managed the environment he was in. He suddenly realised that it was not just about being given his new role, he now needed to *act* his new role – both for himself to give him confidence and for his colleagues so they interacted with him as an equal.

At our next coaching session he described the Executive Team meeting he had just attended and how his contribution had been so much more impactful, and he had felt much happier afterwards. As he fed back to me, I noticed how his energy levels were much higher than before and his language was quite different. He now spoke about what he had been doing, what he had caused to happen, how others had reacted to his contributions rather than sharing his frustration and how he had reacted.

The following is a summary of how you can use this activity with your coaching clients. I always demonstrate it this way when using the model on a coaching skills course.

If possible I do this exercise standing up and literally walk through the various levels, taking a step at a time with my coachee. Over the years I've gradually developed this exercise, and I now tend to use laminated coloured feet to represent the five levels.

I find there is something much more powerful about literally stepping into something rather than imagining that you are doing so. However, if this is not possible due to environmental constraints (with Tom we were sitting in a goldfish bowl office), you can do the activity sitting down and metaphorically walk through the levels, perhaps having a copy of the model in front of you both. One of my coaching students even created a set of mini feet which she placed on the table in front of the coachee and, using a pebble to represent himself, her coachee moved himself up the various levels as they completed the activity. It's an exercise you can do in lots of different ways.

This is one of the few occasions where I do take notes for my coachee as I really want them to experience the activity rather than focussing on capturing their own notes.

ACTIVITY – COACHING SOMEONE THROUGH NEUROLOGICAL LEVELS OF CHANGE

Invite your coachee to think about some kind of change that they would like to happen, and to imagine that it is three or six months' time and that change has happened successfully. Ask them to step into that moment and to answer the questions in figure 9. (Note: the change has already happened, so encourage your coachee to answer in the present tense. For example, instead of answering 'I would be…' Your coachee will be saying 'I am…'.)

Invite your coachee to notice what is different now. What do they notice about themselves? What has caused a shift in their thinking?

I am often asked why the exercise takes you up through the levels and then back down again. The reasoning behind this is that there is a layering effect as you go through the exercise.

I find people generally find it easier to describe their environment or behaviour than they do to describe their identity. It is not a question that we tend to ask ourselves

Figure 9 Neurological Levels of Change Activity

Step forward into IDENTITY

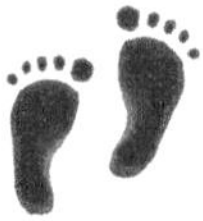

- How would you describe yourself?
- Express this as a metaphor. What symbol or image comes to mind that seems to express your identity?
- Take a small step forward and truly associate with this image of yourself.
- Savour this moment. Notice how you are standing, your posture, your feelings and emotions..

Step forward into BELIEFS & VALUES

- What is important to you?
- What do you believe about yourself and your abilities?

Step forward into SKILLS

- What skills are you using?
- What skills are you particularly noticing yourself drawing upon?

Step forward into BEHAVIOUR

- What are you doing? How would you describe your movements, actions and thoughts? What are others observing you doing?

Step forward into ENVIRONMENT

- Where are you?
- Describe your surroundings. Who is around you? What do you notice particularly about your Environment?

START HERE

Take this image of you as a presenter and turn around so
you are facing the direction you have just come from.

Step forward into BELIEFS & VALUES

- Take the physiology of the Identity level with you.
- What is important to you now?
- What do you believe now?
- What beliefs and values underpin your identity?
- Capture this new sense of your beliefs and values

Step forward into SKILLS

- How are your skills enhanced?
- Are there any additional skills that you are using?

Step forward into BEHAVIOUR

- What do you notice about your behaviour now?
- What are you doing more or less of?
- What are other people noticing?

Step forward into ENVIRONMENT

- What do you notice now about your Environment?

**Take a moment to notice what is different now you
have brought all of these levels of yourself to it.**

every day. Therefore going up the levels in this way is usually easier for people. Once you have described your identity and truly stepped into it, it is amazing how you start to notice new beliefs, skills or behaviour as you go back through the levels. Usually the changes people notice are about new beliefs/skills/behaviour/details of their environment that have now come into focus. Also, if you step into a new, enabling belief as you work your way up the levels, you will definitely notice some changes in the lower order levels as you work your way back down. It is an incredibly powerful exercise and a great way of experiencing neurological levels in action.

I think the most important question facing humanity is, 'Is the universe a friendly place?' This is the first and most basic question all people must answer for themselves.

Einstein

CHAPTER NINE

BUILDING RESILIENCE

As I write this book, at least three of my current coaching clients are practising techniques for building their levels of resilience, and these coaching clients are certainly not alone. Coaching for resilience has been a significant part of my coaching practice over the last few years – probably not surprisingly given the rate of change and increased demands to do more with less, requiring different and often radical ways of working, that are facing most of my coaching clients. 'Resilience' has become a vogue word in coaching. But what exactly is resilience and can we build it?

The Oxford English Dictionary defines resilience as follows:

- The action or an act of rebounding or springing back; rebound, recoil.
- Elasticity: the power of resuming an original shape or position after compression, bending.

In a coaching context, resilience would therefore suggest the ability to bounce back from setbacks. However, this description alone seems too simplistic. The very fact that you are bouncing back assumes that you have been somewhere else in the first place. Something knocked you off course or caused you stress. Understanding what caused this to happen and building strategies to prevent it happening again or minimise its effect next time are therefore important components of building resilience too.

Figure 10 The Stress Response Curve

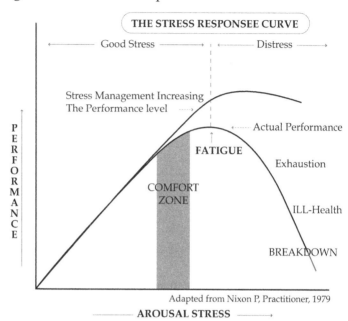

Adapted from Nixon P, Practitioner, 1979

When seeking to understand what resilience is it is useful to understand our responses to stress. Figure 10 demonstrates the stress response curve.

Here an optimal amount of 'good stress', or as it is sometimes called 'eustress', (the 'eu' originating from the Greek *eu* meaning 'well' or 'good'), is required to increase performance levels. However, at some point (which will be different for all of us and dependent on a wide range of factors) eustress will turn to distress. Performance, having plateaued, will start to reduce as fatigue sets in. If distress continues, performance rates may continue to decline, ultimately resulting in ill health. As figure 10 demonstrates, effectively utilising stress management techniques enables performance levels to increase for longer, enabling an individual to continue to perform well under sustained pressure whilst maintaining their own sense of well-being. The model would suggest that, in order to manage our own stress, we need to understand what causes us stress, our responses to it and possibly also learn some new more useful responses.

When explaining resilience, and what it is, to coaching clients, I therefore refer to there being various facets to it. I describe resilience as the ability to:

- Overcome obstacles as they arise
- Steer through everyday adversities
- Bounce back from any setbacks
- Stay open to new challenges and experiences

The good news is we can build our levels of resilience. However, building resilience is not a one-size-fits-all. Thinking back to my own coaching clients, yes, they are all working on building their resilience. However, at face value the challenges they are facing and their coaching outcomes appear to be quite different.

In *The Resilience Factor* Shatté and Reivich provide a useful framework for understanding the different facets of resilience, which they define as: Emotion Regulation, Impulse Control, Optimism, Self-Efficacy, Causal Analysis, Empathy and Reaching Out. I have taken inspiration from this framework and used this to develop a Wheel of Resilience which I use in my own coaching practice. My Wheel of Resilience has eight spokes – I have included the additional element of Interpersonal Confidence – with the following descriptors and definitions.

Self-control. This is about controlling our emotions, keeping anxieties in check and not letting them take over. People who struggle to regulate their emotions do not deal well with setbacks, with unhelpful emotions ranging from getting down or withdrawing from a situation through to angry outbursts. Such individuals can be challenging to work with since others may invest considerable time and energy second guessing how they may react to situations and/or in dealing with their reactions. Conversely people who are good at controlling their emotions are able to manage their responses to challenging situations. They have the ability to express or name an emotion without necessarily showing it. In short, it is not that they do not experience emotions – they manage what they let others see.

Staying focused. This is about doing what is best in the long term, even when it might not be what we want to do. We may be prone to impulse, throwing ourselves into something new and exciting without actually thinking it through. Subsequently we may lose interest and have several 'unfinished' projects on the go. Staying focused therefore reflects 'stickability': keeping commitments and the extent to which we make promises which are achievable – for ourselves and others. Staying focused on the longer-term benefits is the key theme.

Positive Outlook. This is fundamentally the belief that things can and will change for the better. People who are strong in this area believe they have control in the direction of their lives. When faced with setbacks during a project or initiative their natural reaction is to maintain a positive outlook and look for ways to encourage others to stay positive and see the upsides of the situation.

Martin Seligmann's (2000) research suggests that the benefits of an optimistic outlook are many and go beyond the 'feel good' factor, in particular showing strong links to high achievement and overall better health. People who struggle with optimism will present more of a glass half empty perspective to the world and are more likely to give up in the face of adversity.

Self-Belief. This refers to the extent to which we believe we shape what happens to us…or not. Those with strong self-belief believe they can control many aspects of their lives and demonstrate a confidence that they can achieve and make a difference. Each step of progress is viewed as a means of growing knowledge and confidence, and opportunities are sought out to prove the point further. Encountering and overcoming problems increases this sense of self-belief. Those with strong self-belief are not necessarily especially able, but they do believe they have enough ability to do what is required. Those with lower self-belief may avoid doing more or having a go in case they encounter problems.

Maintaining perspective. This is about accurately identifying what is causing the problem and maintaining a sense of perspective. A common trap is to confuse cause and effect, for example the statement 'She makes me angry' where the cause is attributed to someone else. What the speaker is actually experiencing is someone doing something which is causing them to choose to feel angry. The key here is to identify the real cause and accept ownership for the things you can change. Often it is easier to blame someone else and carry on without making a change than to analyse the problem more objectively.

Building empathy. Empathy is the ability to put ourselves into other people's shoes, to see the world through their eyes, to recognise what they are feeling and also appreciate the impact we and/or the situation is having on them. Empathising demonstrates that we understand that the other person has particular feelings, needs or views and that we acknowledge them. However, this is not the same as agreeing. Typical phrases used in displaying empathy are 'I understand you are frustrated' or 'I realise you are finding this situation very upsetting'. Being able to demonstrate empathy, and having an idea how others may respond, increases our chances of positive outcomes since we can anticipate and prepare for situations and adjust our style and approach based on the underlying motivations, needs and style of the person we are working with. A lack of empathy may mean that we appear uninterested or closed to the opinions or viewpoints of others. We may be wrong-footed by an approach that is different to our initial expectations. In the long run we may find ourselves delivering without much support from others.

Interpersonal Confidence. This is the extent to which we are prepared to assert ourselves and to deal with challenge or ridicule. Those with strong interpersonal confidence are more willing to argue their corner, especially if they believe they are in the right, will have a go and enter a conversation and are generally more confident about representing their position on something. This allows them to deal effectively with challenge – they are less likely to be intimidated and will assert themselves in social settings. Those lacking in interpersonal confidence are more likely to back down quickly when challenged or allow others to dominate debates, even when they have more expertise.

Having a go. The title says it all. This is about having a go, doing something different or something differently. People who embrace this component are not afraid of looking stupid or failing, they just want to learn and grow. Energy is not wasted on trying to look perfect or appear as if everything is under control – doing so only increases stress levels, thus reducing resilience.

EXERCISE – MY WHEEL OF RESILIENCE

When working with coachees who are describing problems they are encountering, or outcomes they would like relating to one or more of the eight components described above, I often invite them to complete their Wheel of Resilience with me. (For information on how to create a wheel see Chapter Seven).

The eight components of resilience are represented as spokes of the wheel. Each category of the wheel has a scale of 0–10, with 0 representing a total lack of resilience and 10 representing strong resilience. I talk coachees through each component of resilience and then invite them to shade in the category reflecting the degree to which they feel they have resilience in that part of their life.

Once coachees have completed their wheel I pose the following question: 'If the new perimeter of the wheel represents your Wheel of Resilience, how smooth would the ride be if this were a real wheel?'

I find this exercise always throws up some interesting reflections and observations. Personally I need to make very few comments – perhaps just noticing a high or low score and asking the coachee what that might mean or suggest. Coachees can see for themselves where they currently have high levels of resilience and where these levels are somewhat depleted. As mentioned at the start of this chapter, resilience is not a one-size-fits-all and creating a wheel is a useful way for a coachee to consider:

- What do I need right now?

AND

- What do I already have?

Having completed their wheel, my coachee then selects a component or components that they would like to work on in order to build their level of resilience. To start with I will explore the reasons for their current score and any actions they have tried or could try to increase their score. Useful questions include:

- What are the reasons behind your current score?
- What have you tried so far to improve in this area?
- What have you tried that has worked?
- What have you tried that has not worked?
- What could you do to increase your resilience in this area?
- What else could you try?
- Who do you know that is good at x? What do you notice them doing? How could you apply some of this approach yourself?
- Imagine yourself doing that right now. What do you notice? How could you go about doing that at your next meeting?
- What would happen if you said/did that?
- What would be an alternative response/reaction?
- What opportunities have you got coming up to have a go?

If the coachee is struggling to think of ways of increasing their resilience in a given area I may then share some of my own hints and tips. These comprise of a mixture of exercises, reflections, areas for self-observation that I have collected over the years. These are reproduced on the following pages.

BUILDING RESILIENCE EXERCISES

INCREASING SELF-CONTROL

Take some time to reflect on your current self-control – if you do not know that you are losing it, you will not be able to recognise it. Think about specific situations in which your emotions were triggered in a way that meant you did not deal with the situation in the most effective manner. Think about:

- What was the trigger to the emotion?
- What emotion was triggered?

Write down some strategies for dealing with these emotions next time they are triggered. Think about strategies that are useful for when you need to calm yourself in the moment and also when you can get some time away from the situation to calm yourself.

Practise 'in the moment' techniques including:

- Move in some way. A fixed posture 'holds' the emotion, so it can help you to diffuse the emotion if you consciously do something different.
- Take a couple of deep breaths to help relax the muscles in the body. The key is to breathe out a little more than you would normally. The breath you take in will then be naturally deeper and, as you let it out slowly, the calming effect will be experienced.
- Count to ten. If you have ever spoken in anger you know that it is possible to react to a situation when your emotion is triggered by saying something that is not helpful, which you then regret. Pausing helps you to think – you can then choose a more considered response.
- Say how you feel. This is effective if you do it assertively, channelling some of the energy of the emotion into what you say, but avoiding using emotive words. For example, you could say: 'I'm finding this frustrating because...'

- Buy some time. Get away from the situation so that you can use more time to manage the emotion. E.g., 'I need to talk to you more about this, but I have something urgent I need to deal with right now. Could we talk again in...?'
- Concentrate on the positives. Scan your day and note down three 'good' things, or things that have gone well for you. Review these at the end of the week. What themes are emerging? What are you noticing about yourself?
- Reframe the situation. This means thinking about the situation from a different point of view, especially the point of view of the other person in a disagreement. Put yourself in their shoes. You may need to have some time to calm yourself by other means first. However, when you are able to, it will help to change the emotion. For example, in the moment we often feel that someone is being deliberately awkward, but after some thought we often realise that they were having a difficult time, or had not realised the effect of their behaviour.

STAYING FOCUSED

Be more aware of your immediate reaction to things. Is it the most appropriate? Will it have the best long-term outcome?

Urgent versus important. Few tasks are actually both urgent and important. We confront 'urgent' problems all the time and they assume importance because they seem to demand immediate action. As a result far too many important tasks only get done when they become urgent as well. Practise the art of prioritising, making and, as far as possible, adhering to 'to do' lists. Be really clear about making time for, and sticking to, tasks which are important but not urgent. These will often be key to our long term performance, e.g. KPIs, objectives, projects, etc. Focus on dealing with urgent tasks quickly to allow time for the important tasks.

DEVELOPING A POSITIVE OUTLOOK

Be more consciously aware of your own negative attributions/ pessimistic style, e.g. 'all or none thinking', 'yes, but' responses, etc. People who are more negative tend to explain their adversities with a 'me, always, everything' style. Optimists, by contrast, tend to have a 'not-me, not-always, not-everything' style. Tune up your awareness, notice the language you use, both your internal self-talk and what you say to others. Ask others to provide you with feedback.

Practise the technique of one door closes and another door opens. Focus on what new opportunities are available now. Where can you refocus your energy? What is the upside of this decision/result?

Practise goal setting and putting into place strategies for attaining personal goals, thereby reducing negative expectations. Break big goals into stepping goals or smaller sub goals and quick wins.

DEVELOPING SELF-BELIEF

Recall a time when you overcame a problem you were not expecting. What did you do? How did you set about overcoming the problem? How did you feel when you overcame it? How can you use this insight in the future?

Take some time to list your strengths or take a strengths inventory to assess them against a model. What key strengths do you have? How can you use these more or in different ways?

Recall a past success, one of which you're particularly proud. Note down the skills, behaviours, etc. that you employed to make this occasion a successful one.

Who do you know that comes across as self-confident? Consider what they do, say and believe. What can you learn from observing others? How can you employ some of these strategies yourself?

Future pace yourself. Imagine a future scenario which has been a great success based upon significant input from you. Imagine that scenario is happening right now. What are you seeing, hearing and feeling? What are you noticing about the self-confident you in action?

MAINTAINING PERSPECTIVE

As touched on above in 'Developing a Positive Outlook', become consciously aware of your thinking patterns, i.e. the habitual way you explain the good and bad things that happen to you. Everyone's explanatory style can be coded on three dimensions: personal ('me/ not me'), permanent ('always/not always') and pervasive ('everything/ not everything') ways of thinking. A 'me, always, everything' person automatically believes that he/she caused the problem (me), that it is lasting and unchangeable (always) and that it will pervade all aspects of his/her life (everything). By contrast, when a problem arises a 'not me, not always, not everything' person believes that other people or circumstances caused the problem (not me), that it is temporary and changeable (not always) and that it will not affect all of their life (not everything). The two people described will interpret the same situation very differently. Consider your thinking pattern. What is your habitual style? Does this serve you well? Check yourself when something doesn't go as well as you'd like. What do you find yourself thinking and saying to yourself? Practise changing the words and notice the effect this has.

Think about an issue that is concerning you. What really causes that issue? What do you do that might not help or which adds to the problem? What can you change?

BUILDING EMPATHY

Set aside some time, for example at the end of your day, to review whether you were engaged appropriately at any level of empathy.

Notice what happened in terms of specific behaviours. The following prompts may be useful:

- Did you listen when someone approached you to express feelings? Or did you feel too busy to talk about such things and brush the person off?
- Did you practise using open-ended probes, such as 'Tell me more about that', to make sure you understood the other person's point of view fully, as to both emotion and content?
- Did you adjust your style and approach based on the needs and style of the person you were working with – for example, through body language (gestures, posture), tonality (tone, pitch, speed, volume), dress (formality) and environment (space, formality)?
- Did you understand underlying motivations for others' behaviour (recognise they come from different backgrounds, have different values and beliefs) and adjust your response accordingly?

Keep a log of situations in which you feel you demonstrated empathy and situations in which you did not. Pay particular attention to critical incidents that provided opportunities for you to:

- Identify underlying concerns that were not explicitly stated by others
- Hear the emotions that accompanied an expressed statement.

Imagine a future meeting/event with another person. Step into their shoes. What is important to them? What motivates them? What might be worrying them? What can you do to impact on them in a positive way?

When interacting with others, be open to their opinions and viewpoints. Adapt your own responses to others' needs and be willing to accept an outcome that may be different from your initial expectations. Understanding and adapting to others' needs will increase your effectiveness.

BUILDING INTERPERSONAL CONFIDENCE

Think about the situations where you feel you don't speak out and assert your position. Use your next few internal meetings to experiment with different styles and approaches. Analyse how you felt each time and how each style was received.

Develop a diary/planning journal that will identify asserting yourself and speaking out opportunities, useful questions, influence attempts/ outcomes, and include a continue to do/do more analysis section. Discuss strategies and results with others, preferably a person who has demonstrated interpersonal confidence with others.

Practise the Stating Your Position Activity

- Think of something that you would like to recommend/ propose/change at work.
- Select three key reasons to support your recommendation/ proposal/suggestion. Focus on quality, not quantity.
- Write down the exact words you would use, starting with 'I suggest...', 'I think...', or 'I recommend...'
- Consider the exact choice of words, your tone and your body language to maximise your impact
- Practise using the technique in some key meetings and notice what happens.

Decide for a day/a week to speak out in meetings and assert your position without being fearful of challenge or ridicule. Invent an internal separation in yourself. Divide yourself into two persons, one who acts/reacts in life and one who observes and is passive in life. Using the following questions, begin to observe yourself in life. Observe quietly, passively. Observe your internal state as well as what you show the world. At the end of the day, scan through your day and note what happened and how you reacted. You may want to write notes so you can begin to notice patterns.

- In what ways did you assert your position in relationships, conversations, meetings?
- What happened when you asserted yourself? How did you feel? Did it produce any challenge/conflict/ridicule? How did you respond to this?
- Did you feel like speaking out and asserting your position and not do it? How are you justifying that? What were the consequences of not pushing back, especially in terms of your emotions, mood and energy?
- What are you learning about yourself, speaking out and asserting your position? How and when will you take your learning into action?

HAVING A GO

Try doing something new – it may be as basic as asking for some help. You may choose to take on a project you normally would have avoided. The question to ask yourself is: what's the worst thing that can happen? Usually the answer is not as bad as we fear.

How would you describe yourself? Are you more achievement oriented, acceptance oriented or control oriented? Take a moment and reflect – when you find yourself shrinking from opportunities is it out of a fear of failure, concerns over rejection or worries about not being in control? Think about something that you'd like to do, but haven't so far. What is stopping you? What limiting beliefs are you holding? What would it be useful to believe instead? Step into that belief and have a go. Take some time after to reflect on what that was like.

Decide for a day/a week to be open and curious to any and all possibilities and to let go of any attachment to specific outcomes.

Invent an internal separation in yourself. Divide yourself into two persons, one who acts/reacts in life and one who observes and is passive in life. Using the following questions, begin to observe yourself in life. Observe quietly, passively. Observe your internal state as well as what you show the world. At the end of the day, scan through your day and note what happened and how you reacted. You may want to write notes so you can begin to notice patterns.

- In what ways were you open and curious today?
- What happened when you were open and curious? How did you feel?
- Did you hold back and decide not to have a go at something? How are you justifying that to yourself/others? What were the consequences of you holding back, especially in terms of your emotions, mood and energy?
- What are you learning about yourself and being open and curious? How and when will you take your learning into action?

Finally, as coaches I believe it is also incumbent on us to reflect on what we do and what we model in our coaching sessions. Do we positively expand our coachees' thinking repertoires and, in so doing, help build their resilience? Do we challenge and raise our coachees' awareness of negative language and attributions, e.g. all or nothing thinking? Do we evoke positive emotion in our coachees? Do we increase positive expectations about outcomes, e.g. supporting coachees in practising strategies to attain personal goals (thereby reducing negative expectations)? Do we present a can-do attitude? Equally, do we help our coachees develop a staunch view of reality by reframing setbacks; encouraging realistic assessment of setbacks in terms of impact control and options, and supporting the process of learning, insight, growth and development from setbacks and mistakes?

What do we role model in our coaching practice? Do we provide space, support, challenge and quality reflection, so enabling our coachees to re-energise and reinvigorate?

We cannot solve our problems with the same level of thinking that created them.

Albert Einstein

CHAPTER TEN

A CREATIVE APPROACH TO MANAGING RELATIONSHIPS

If you are already a practising coach I am sure you have had occasions when you have found your coachee 'stuck'. Perhaps you find yourself listening at length to the coachee's narrative, yet sensing that somehow they need to move below the surface to explore the real issue. If you're new to coaching you may equally be concerned as to what to do if your coachee gets 'stuck'. Using non-cognitive and creative approaches can be incredibly useful in enabling coachees to gain insight into the dynamics of a situation that they are caught up in. Using creative tools frees the coachee to explore, gaining knowledge through perceptions and insights, rather than through their analytical mind.

In addition, everyone has their own unique way of learning and working. An individual's learning style influences how they take in information and how they communicate. There are many theories about how people learn, including that individuals have sensory learning styles. The Sensory Learning Styles Model suggests that individuals have preferences for using one or more of their senses when paying attention and processing information. Although there are five senses, there are generally considered to be three dominant sensory learning styles: visual, auditory and kinaesthetic (covering touch, taste and smell). These are summarised below:

- **Visual.** Has a preference for pictures, photos, diagrams and other visual props. Likes to watch a demonstration or visualise an experience.
- **Auditory.** Appreciates the opportunity to discuss things, enjoys asking questions. Appreciates being listened to.
- **Kinaesthetic.** Enjoys 'doing' things. Appreciates being hands on, tactile, having a go. Likes the message to be set in a personal context.

Whilst we all do all of the above, most of us usually have a preference for two of the styles and will often access their least-preferred style through one of the other two. For example, I may be predominantly visual and kinaesthetic and access my least preferred style, auditory, through one of these channels. In order to hear the sound of my alarm clock I may first need to visualise the clock and then access the sound of the alarm. (For a more in-depth explanation of visual, auditory and kinaesthetic, see *Presenting Yourself with Impact*, 2010).

I believe the Sensory Learning Styles Model has some important implications for coaching. Much 'traditional' coaching is largely auditory – asking questions, listening to responses and asking follow up questions. However, my own experience of working with individuals is that few people have auditory as their strongest preference. The majority of people tell me that the visual style is their strongest preference, closely followed by kinaesthetic.

Over the years I have found that I've gravitated away from simply asking questions towards using a range of tools, techniques and specific questions that encourage coachees to use other sensory preferences. The wheels, described in Chapters Seven and Nine, are of course very visual tools. Coachees complete them and can see for themselves – if this were a wheel, how smooth would my ride be? The neurological levels exercise described in Chapter Eight ticks all of the boxes. It's a visual exercise – you can see the levels as you walk up them. The use of questions appeals to the auditory preference. Additionally it's also very kinaesthetic, encouraging the coachee to step into the levels and experience the change and how that feels right now. So we have already covered a number of different techniques and this chapter introduces some additional multi-sensory and creative tools.

As I mentioned in the Introduction, I was introduced to a range of creative coaching supervision processes whilst I was studying for my coaching supervision diploma with the CSA. As part of this process I started working with a coach supervisor, Alison Hodge, who specialises in using creative approaches in her work. I subsequently joined a creative coaching supervision group which exposed me to a wealth of techniques for working with others in a more creative fashion, many of which I have now integrated into my coaching practice.

This chapter introduces a 'tapas' of creative tools and techniques that I use with coachees when a coachee is wanting to explore the dynamics of a relationship – perhaps a conflict situation with someone, or a tricky relationship with a team member or colleague.

MAGIC BOX

Originally introduced to me by the CSA, and perhaps my favourite technique, 'Magic Box' is the technique I use most often. With its origins in Gestalt Therapy, Magic Box is a way of choosing and placing objects on a surface so that relationships between people and patterns become obvious, dialogue between players can be facilitated and resolutions to tricky situations, or where a person feels 'stuck', start to become clearer. Magic Box is particularly useful if there are multiple players in the situation where the coachee currently feels stuck. At face value the activity does look a little odd – and I have certainly had some very strange looks from my coachees when I have suggested using it, and even stranger looks when I have then opened my own Magic Box. However, I have found that for the majority of my coachees it helps them get out of their heads. It stops them over-thinking about something and gives them permission to 'play' – typically something we do not do a lot of at work.

To use Magic Box you first need to create one. To do so collect a variety of small objects – buttons, shells, dice, plastic animals, feathers, stones, pebbles, etc. and a container to put them in. I discovered a small leather briefcase which had belonged to my dad languishing in my mum's shed. It's a bit battered and worn and oozes history and experience and is absolutely perfect for this exercise. When using the exercise you first need to create a surface with a clear boundary. This could be the table top or a piece of flipchart paper. I tend to use a linen napkin which I keep in my Magic Box.

When introducing the activity to coaching clients I ask them if they fancy doing something a bit different, perhaps having a play with a few ideas, perhaps getting out of their heads for a little time. If they say yes (and in my experience they always do) I will then lightly mention that the activity will look a little different but to bear with me before I produce my Magic Box and open it up.

To start with I ask the coachee to name the issue they want to explore, for example the tricky relationship they have with a particular colleague. I then spread the napkin out in front of the coachee and explain that this is the landscape that we will be using for the activity. The exercise then proceeds as follows:

Invite the coachee to choose an object which somehow represents them in this situation and to place it somewhere on the napkin. Throughout the activity as a coach you need to use a light touch. I always use a style of curiosity and enquiry. When they have placed the item I will lightly enquire what it is about the item they have chosen that reminds them of themselves.

Next invite the coachee to choose an object that somehow represents the other person, the one they have the tricky relationship with. Once this item is chosen and placed, again lightly ask what it is about that item.

Continue with this process until all the key players have been chosen and placed. I usually continue to probe – 'Is there anyone else? Who else needs to be represented?' Take time with each item to explore what is represented by this particular object. You will notice that the coachee's reflections, insights and observations deepen as the process develops. Continue until the coachee is clear that the landscape is complete.

The following step again needs a light touch. Invite your coachee to take a look at their landscape and comment on what they notice, what strikes them about it. Typically people will comment on where items are placed in relation to each other, who is standing close or far away from whom, the size of items in relation to each other, who is facing whom, who has their back to whom, who is standing up, who is lying down. At the end I may offer up some of my own observations or question what may be the significance of something, but only when the coachee has given their own reflections.

Having reflected on the current landscape, you then enquire, 'So what needs to happen?' You can add further prompts, for example, 'Do any of the items need to be changed?' 'Do any of the items need to move?' Again, typically coachees know what needs to happen and will often immediately change an item (usually themselves) and/or move items either closer together or further apart.

Once the landscape has been remodelled you then start to draw the activity to a close by asking the coachee what insights they have about what needs to happen. What actions do they need to take? Often these actions will take the form of conversations that need to happen, for example, 'Well Spikey Hedgehog (an object they've chosen to represent themself) needs to have a conversation with Ball (the other person)'.

I may well follow up on this comment with 'And what will Spikey Hedgehog say?' I may even suggest that that conversation takes place right now. The exercise does tend to take on a life of its own, and so as a coach I tend just to go with where the energy is, be guided by my coachee and offer up light enquiry. I may also make a few notes for my client as they are likely to be too preoccupied to do so.

Once you have a sense that your coachee is 'done' – and you will know when they are – invite them to take a photograph or drawing of their landscape. I find that many clients like to do this as a visual reminder of the activity. Once they have done this invite your coachee to return their items to the Magic Box. I always let the coachee do this, being mindful that they invested quite a lot of themselves into some of the items.

With all items safely returned to the Magic Box I will then have a wider reflection on the activity with my coachee, including how they found the activity, what they liked about it, what popped up for them, what surprised them.

One of the additional benefits I have found of Magic Box is that the learning goes on long after the activity has ended. I have had many coaching clients who have continued to refer to the activity in following sessions, often referring to the items they chose. For example, 'Spikey Hedgehog hasn't returned, Smooth Pebble is still at work.' The nice thing is the coachee knows exactly what they mean, and I have a very good insight too. We have developed our own shorthand.

MAGIC BOX IN ACTION

It was my third coaching session with Harriet. Harriet had mentioned at a previous session her tendency to get too involved in other people's problems. She had a friendly engaging personality and a genuine desire to help others – which meant that other people tended to bring their problems to her and she typically ended up trying to resolve them for them. We had mentioned Magic

Box at our previous session, and Harriet had expressed an interest in using it next time.

Before we started I asked Harriet to name the issue she wanted to explore. She described her issue as 'managing boundaries and my tendency to get too involved'. She had a recent situation that she wanted to explore as an example of the above.

Harriet immediately appeared at ease with the exercise. She dived into the Magic Box and started placing items on the linen napkin – a key for herself to denote her 'unlocking the situation'; a large dice for her client who 'is boxed in'; a small frog for Harriet's friend, 'the only person I've confided in' – until all the players were in place as captured in figure 11.

I then asked Harriet what she noticed. The revelation was immediate and powerful.

'Oh my God, everything is in one corner. I'm boxed in; I'm not acting as a key at all. The only person near me is the frog and they're not even in the organisation. There are people there who shouldn't be.' Harriet paused and continued to stare at her landscape.

'So what needs to happen?' I asked. Again the answer was immediate. Harriet replaced the key with a ball.

'This makes me more nimble, I can move about'. She placed herself in the middle of the napkin and firmly and deliberately removed 'the others who shouldn't be there but get involved'.

In a matter of minutes Harriet had gained a new perspective on how she managed boundaries in her work. (See figure 12). Reflecting later, Harriet commented

Figure 11 Harriet's Landscape

Figure 12 Harriet's Remodelled Landscape

that 'I'm not sure I'd have got to that realisation just using words. It would have taken so much longer.'

My experience with Harriet provided two early and very powerful lessons about creativity. My first lesson was that creative approaches can be very quick interventions – the whole activity took less than ten minutes. It would have taken much longer if we had sat and discussed what might have been going on.

The second lesson came a little later. At the start of the next session, Harriet volunteered, 'I experienced a sense of clarity last time. I felt the tools had tapped into my psyche. The visual images were powerful and they've stayed with me. It was hugely thought-provoking and challenging. I've been thinking about how I compartmentalise things. I think I experience things and move on, but I've been wondering, do I put it in a box and move on? I think I do this a fair bit. I put it in a box and move on…But it hasn't gone away, it's still there…' And so my second lesson was that creative approaches can be incredibly powerful. The intervention may have long been over, but the learning continues.

STORYTELLING CUBES AND CARDS

I use a number of different storytelling techniques in my coaching, including storytelling cubes and cards.

Storytelling cubes are versatile tools which can be used as a warm-up activity, to fire up your coachee's imagination prior to another activity or as an activity in their own right. I use Rory's Story Cubes by the Creativity Hub. There are a number of sets of cubes, including Actions, Voyages and Random, which you can use on their own or you can mix and match them. It's easy to make up your own activities, e.g. roll the nine cubes and then make up a story connecting all of the cubes starting with 'Once upon a time…'

Through my supervisor, I have also been introduced to metaphoric associative storytelling cards. The ones I use are by the artist Ely Raman. There are a range of cards, including Saga, OH, Mythos, Ecco, Persona and Personita. The first four are different series of abstract and mythical cards. The final two have a range of figures on them as well as a separate set of relationship cards. (More details are available from the OH Cards Institute (*http://www.OH-Cards-Institute.org*)

I use the Saga and Mythos cards in a similar way to the storytelling cubes, inviting my coachee to select three cards either 'blind' (not looking at them first) or spreading them out and quickly selecting the three cards they are first drawn to. I then invite my coachee to tell a story connecting their three cards starting with 'Once upon a time…'

Whilst the story may have no obvious relevance to the issue my coachee is wrestling with, I've found that my coachee invariably finds a link when they reflect on the story they have just told. There's an interesting nugget in there to explore. Popova and Miloradova writing on the OH Cards Institute website explain the theory behind this.

> *Our unconscious always knows the right thing to do, how to find a way out of the situation, and what choice to make; it is only necessary to learn to listen to it. Metaphoric associative cards, in this case, are an indispensable guide and assistant.*

186

I have a range of activities using associative storytelling cards – some that Alison has introduced me to and others that I have developed myself. The following activity is one I often use when someone wants to explore the dynamics of a tricky relationship with someone else. Those of you who have done some training in NLP will recognise that the activity is based on the parts integration exercise.

Clive was telling me about the relationship with one of his team members. He was feeling stuck. He tried to explain the situation to me and we both become stuck in the narrative. I felt as if Clive needed to get out of his head, to let go of the conscious and let the unconscious mind do the work for a change. I suggested trying something a bit different to Clive and he readily agreed.

I spread the Persona cards out over the table face up and invited Clive to choose a card that represented himself in this relationship. He chose a picture of an old man with a white beard. 'I'm the wise old man, the sage, the teacher in this relationship'. He then picked up a picture of a woman smiling. 'This is Elena, she's the pupil. We're too much pupil and teacher'.

I then invited Clive to choose a card from the dynamic card pack that somehow represented their relationship. He chose one of two circles with lots of arrows between them going backwards and forwards. 'This represents her dumping on me and me teaching. It doesn't flow'.

There was a long pause whilst we both studied the cards. 'What would you like the relationship to be like?' I asked.

Clive immediately picked up another dynamic card showing three dots and two arrows. 'This represents me enabling Elena and Elena enabling her team'.

Figure 13 Clive and Elena's Relationship

I then asked what parts of Clive needed to be added to shift this relationship. He added four more faces which he said for him represented creativity, different and new perspectives for Clive to bring into their meetings. I asked the same for Elena and he added two cards, one very red and one blue. Clive explained that his company used the Insights Discovery Personality Profiling System and that the red card represented more fiery red energy, which he felt Elena needed to get the job done. The blue represented the cooler, logical, rational Elena, which Clive felt Elena should use more.

Within ten minutes we had moved from a conversation which seemed to be going round in circles to Clive surfacing some powerful insights about the dynamics of the relationship. We concluded the session by 'future pacing' to Clive's next one-to-one with Elena the following week. What needed to happen? How did Clive need to be in order to facilitate the above?

USING PHOTOGRAPHS/POSTCARDS

However, you don't need to buy specialist cards to use, and I think you can have a lot of fun creating your own materials. At Iridium we have collected approximately 400 photographs over the years, and I use these extensively with my coaching clients and also in coaching workshops.

I typically spread the photographs over a coffee table and invite my coachee to choose at least one photograph which represents their relationship with the person they are struggling with. Invariably they'll choose more than one photo. Once they've done this I'll ask them to explain why they chose these photos and what they say about this particular relationship. For example, my coachee might say, 'Well I've chosen this one here, I think it's of two rhinos locking horns. That's how it feels in this relationship. It's always a tussle, neither of us wanting to lose.'

Once we've explored the current situation I invite my coachee to choose at least one which represents how they would like this relationship to be and again to explain why they've chosen what they've chosen. For example, my coachee might say, 'I've chosen this one of a surfer riding a wave. Not really sure why, other than that it looks effortless. I'd like this relationship not to be as hard work, to feel effortless.'

This may then lead on to a conversation as to what needs to happen for the relationship to feel 'effortless'. In particular, what does the coachee need to do? What do they need to change? Since, after all, they are the one sitting in this room and the only person that they can actually change. The conversation could then take numerous courses. For example, 'Well I could be more flexible like this person' (picking up the picture of the woman practising yoga).

'It's occurred to me that our interactions have a familiar pattern to them. They voice their opinion without asking mine. I push back with my opinion. I hear them say "Yes, but…" without actually listening to what I have to say and then reiterate what they want. So…I could practise doing something different…maybe not immediately disagreeing with them…Maybe asking a few questions…'

The rest of the coaching session may be spent exploring strategies for the coachee to try out in future and planning when to put these into practice.

You can either put together your own photograph collection, as I have done, or purchase sets of postcards. The Maverick postcards are a great selection of unusual postcards and can be purchased online. I also pick up unusual postcards on my travels. I collected some whilst working in Shanghai recently. These postcards are unusual and had the added benefit of picturing scenes and people that looked familiar to my audience, who were all Chinese.

DRAWING

I always make sure I have a stash of plain paper and coloured pens to hand just in case. On a number of occasions my coachee has started to explain something by sketching on a piece of paper. Alternatively, if they're struggling to describe something in words, I may invite them to take a few minutes to narrate their 'issue' and then draw a picture based on this issue. Sometimes I may even draw the picture that is emerging for me at the same time and we can both share our pictures and how we've experienced the story. Others ways of drawing include mind maps or interaction diagrams. Anything goes really – if it makes sense to your coachee and helps shape their thinking. Debriefing the drawing is the interesting part. What shapes, colours and sizes has the coachee used and what is the significance of these? What picture is emerging? What is your coachee taking away from the activity?

METAPHORS

Of course, being creative does not always need to be about using physical tools and objects to stimulate imagination and intuition. Expressive media (stories, images and metaphors) can be equally rich and insightful. In one memorable session with my supervision triad I shared how I felt I was acting as a 'super coach' rather than a supervisor with one of my supervisees. The person who was supervising me asked me to describe a 'super coach'. I couldn't find the words.

Seamlessly, she asked, 'If you were an instrument or animal as a super coach what would you be?'

After a slight pause, I replied, 'A double bass, sitting behind my supervisee who's a cello.'

'And what do you do as a double bass?' she asked.

'I play the notes lower, at a different pitch. I sit behind them...'

'And what would you like to be?' she enquired.

'A piccolo. I'd be sitting in a different section of the orchestra, having a different perspective, playing a different part at a different pitch...'

Within minutes I'd articulated the difference between 'super coach' and 'supervisor'. Accessing my imagination had enabled fresh insight into the dynamics of the relationship I was caught up in. I experienced at first-hand how, within the metaphor, there's often a creative solution already there just waiting to reveal itself.

So metaphors and analogies are a great way of accessing the imagination and gaining fresh insights on a situation. Sometimes I may adopt a 'clean' approach and invite my coachee to choose their own metaphor by using the clean language question: 'And that...is like what...?' (See Chapter Four for an explanation of clean language.) On other occasions I might offer my coachee a metaphor, especially if they are struggling to express themselves.

The dance metaphor is a very popular metaphor in coaching and can give rise to some interesting discussions with regard to the actual dance, the steps, who is leading and who is following, etc. Some of my other favourite metaphors when exploring tricky relationships with a coachee are:

- What animal are you/the other person in this relationship?
- If you and the other person were instruments in an orchestra what instruments would you be?
- When you and the other person are together what game/sport do you play?
- What kind of circus act are you and the other person? What kind of circus act would you like to be?
- What kind of steps are you and the other person taking? (E.g. short steps, big strides, walking in the snow taking careful short steps, etc.)

If I know my coachee has a particular interest, hobby or pastime I might offer this up as a metaphor. One recent example was with Paul.

Paul was telling me about his relationship with a member of his team. This person was very capable, and Paul saw him as potentially having a bright future with the company. However, Paul felt that the two of them didn't work together as well as they could, but Paul was struggling to put his finger on quite what the problem was. I knew Paul was a keen cricketer, and so asked him, 'If you and X were playing cricket together, what would that be like?'

Paul paused and thought for a moment and then responded, 'Well we'd be batting together and we'd both be doing well and building big scores. However, every time we ran between the wickets there'd be a danger that one of us would run the other one out. We wouldn't be working together…we'd both be concentrating on our own game…'

Finally Paul had put his finger on the problem. There was too much competition and not enough collaboration in the relationship and we seamlessly moved on to what Paul could do to start to change the relationship.

The above are just a small selection of some of the creative methods I've discovered can be useful in coaching. The nice thing about creative methods is that, once you get started, once you get used to playing, the possibilities are endless. I'm now constantly on the look-out for ideas, objects, pictures, games that I can use in my coaching. Our holiday photographs make interesting viewing these days, and Christmas cracker gifts often find a home in my Magic Box. If you're not already experimenting with creative techniques I'd encourage you to. It's enormous fun and brings a real richness and different dimension to your coaching.

*Out beyond ideas of wrong doing and
right doing there is a field.
I'll meet you there.*

**Rumi,
Thirteenth Century Sufi Poet**

CHAPTER ELEVEN

EMOTIONAL INTELLIGENCE AND A TRANSACTIONAL ANALYSIS APPROACH TO MANAGING RELATIONSHIPS

In his research on what constitutes emotional intelligence and its significance to relationships at work, Daniel Goleman concluded that there were four tenets of emotional intelligence: self-awareness, self-management, social awareness and relationship management. The model Goleman developed demonstrates how self-awareness, self-control and social awareness competencies all feed into relationship management, as demonstrated in figure 14.

Without accurate self-awareness our ablity to forge and maintain good relationships at work is, Goleman argues, significantly compromised. Whilst coachees may not necessary articulate their goal as a need to develop their self-awareness, I find much of my time coaching is spent enabling coachees gain a more accurate picture of their strengths, weaknesses and impact on others. Many of the tools and techniques already described in this book, including personality questionnaires, the wheels, values elicitation, neurological levels of change, strengths inventories and 360° feedback are useful for developing self-awareness. I have therefore chosen to explore

Figure 14 The Four Tenets of Emotional Intelligence

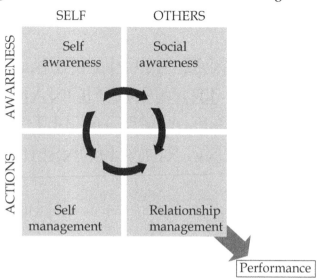

self-awareness as a theme throughout the book rather than as the subject of a specific chapter.

Whilst I have had people come for coaching with specific outcomes for improving their self-awareness, regulating their emotions at work or developing their organisational awareness/political savvy, far more frequently people come for coaching wanting to improve how they manage relationships at work – be it leading, influencing, coaching or collaborating with others or navigating their way through conflict. In working with managing relationships issues, I find Transactional Analysis (TA) a useful framework to help the coachee, and me, understand what may be going on psychologically in the tricky relationship the coachee finds themselves in. With some coachees I may share the TA framework, particularly if this person likes models and frameworks and wants to understand what is going on with situations. With other coachees, who I know are not fond of models or who may have made comments such as 'I don't like psychobabble' during our contracting conversation, I may not describe the nitty-gritty of the framework, but use it more as a framework to inform me what may be going on in the dynamics of the relationship that the coachee is describing.

The theory of TA was developed by Eric Berne in the 1950s. In essence Berne suggested that when we communicate with others we do so from one of three ego states: Parent, Adult or Child. The three states are summarised below:

Parent. The Parent ego state utilises attitudes and behaviour patterns which resemble those of a parental figure, borrowed or modelled. When we are in Parent state we can behave in two ways – controlling/disciplining/restricting or nurturing/helpful/caring/maternal. The controlling Parent state is categorised by words such as right/wrong; good/bad; never/always; you should/shouldn't; in my experience. The Nurturing Parent state, by contrast, uses expressions such as: what a shame; take care; remember to; come here and I'll help you; leave it to me. The Parent state comes from our experiences of life with our parents and teachers, particularly in early life. When we feel, think, talk and behave in the way we remember our parents doing then we are adopting a Parent state. Often it is the attitudes rather than the actual words that reveal themselves in later life. Consider the following expressions spoken by a coach:

- 'In my experience as a coach...' (Controlling Parent)
- 'Leave it to me... ' (Nurturing Parent)

Child. The Child ego state utilises attitudes and behaviour patterns which are relics of our own childhood. In

Child state we can also act in one of two ways – Free Child or Adapted Child. Free Child is categorised by impulsive, instinctive, creative, undisciplined and, at times, demanding behaviour. Adapted Child is when we carry the influences of our upbringing, for example doing as we are told, into the present day. Such behaviour may give rise to guilt, rebellion, obedience or compromise.

Adult. The Adult ego state utilises feelings, attitudes and behaviour patterns which are adapted to current reality. In essence it is us, operating in the present, here and now. The Adult ego is the mature and deliberating part of personality and so actions and words are sensible and well-considered. The Adult state focuses on collecting information, evaluating it, working out possibilities and resolving problems in a logical, calm way. It concentrates on facts – not feelings or prejudices. When we are in Adult state our actions and words are well considered – in contrast to the almost automatic reactions of the Parent or Child states.

All of us have access to these three states and we use different ones at different times. They can all be useful, have their strengths and weaknesses and are appropriate in different circumstances. We are, however, likely to have preferred states or a tendency to adopt some more than others. It is the balance between the three that is said to make up our personality.

EXERCISE – MY EGO STATES

Take a moment and write down your immediate responses to the following five statements:

- A recent time when you took care of someone
- A recent time when you made somebody do something that they didn't want to do

- When you have a task to complete, two or three things you do to complete that task effectively
- Two or three things you do when you want to be noticed
- Two or three things you do for pleasure/fun/joy/happiness

Now, either on your own or with a partner, consider your responses. Which ego state have you answered each question from? Were there some states you used more than others? Others that you did not use?

TA terminology identifies two forms of transactions that we can have – complementary and crossed.

Complementary transactions proceed smoothly because both parties are using states that are expected to be used. These transactions can use any of the three states, as demonstrated in figure 15.

However, crossed transactions occur when one party uses a state that was not expected, and that is when we can get into conflict and difficulties. An example of crossed transactions is shown in figure 16.

TA is, I believe, a useful model to explore in coaching – both in developing ourselves and our own coaching practice and when working with coachees and helping them explore their own patterns of behaviour and some of the challenging conversations they are having with others.

Firstly, as coaches it is important that, as much as possible, we keep our coaching conversations 'Adult'. 'Adult' coaching behaviours would include:

Being respectful, including giving real time and attention to someone. Contracting is an Adult-to-Adult conversation, so we need to ensure that we contract with the 'Adult' in our client.

Having a confident appearance – our posture, tone of voice, body language.

Encouraging the coachee to take ownership of the issue and suggest their own solutions.

If we give feedback to the coachee, it should be done from a non-judgemental position, making it considered with specifics and examples and based on facts, not personality.

Being alert to our coachee pulling us into an ego state, for example, their Child pulling us into Nurturing Parent.

Using inclusive language, for example 'we, us, let's' rather than 'I need/you must'.

Secondly the TA Ego States can be useful for exploring with our coachees particularly difficult relationships. For example:

What is going on in the relationship?

How do you feel when you are interacting with this person?

Figure 15 Complementary Transactions

Figure 16 A Crossed Transaction

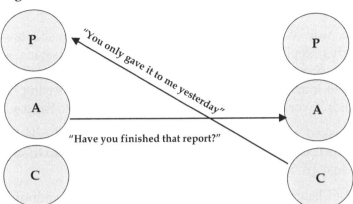

"You only gave it to me yesterday"

"Have you finished that report?"

How old do you feel when you are interacting with this person?

What words/expressions do you/the other party typically use? How might these words/expressions be perceived by the other party?

What do you need to do to have an Adult-to-Adult conversation with this person?

It was my first coaching session with Paula. I asked her what she wanted to discuss and she immediately stated that she had someone who was a delegate on a training course she was running who was 'un-coachable'. Stephen, the 'un-coachable', was, she said, reluctant to commit to any learning or development outcomes, but Paula had received feedback from other delegates and his boss that his style could be irritating. In Paula's words, 'He puts himself forward as Mr Perfect and constantly tells everyone what a great job he's doing'. Paula felt she had a dilemma – she could stay safe, go through the motions and fulfil her contract. Stephen was happy with that, but she felt that it would be compromising her own values.

By way of illustration, Paula recounted a recent situation when Stephen had left a feedback session with her saying he was going to try something out. It didn't work for him, and he'd immediately sent Paula a 'childish' email, saying, 'It didn't work, they're idiots, just what I expected to happen'.

I asked what impact this email had had on Paula, to which she replied, 'It was childish, petty, I wanted to say, "Just grow up!"'

As I listened to the language Paula used, I was mindful that in transactional analysis terminology Paula was describing Stephen's behaviour in 'Adapted Child' terms and she was sounding very much like a 'Controlling Parent'. I felt I needed to tap into the 'Adult' in Paula. I was also mindful of Paula's initial outcome, that she had explained when we'd contracted, of providing more challenge in her work.

'How could she do this from "Adult"?' I wondered.

I held the silence, and then asked, 'What would happen if you told him the effect his email had on you?'

At this point Paula's physiology changed dramatically. She sat upright. 'You're right,' she said. She went on to say how she needed to work on the robustness of the relationship. Stephen had received feedback from his 360° feedback that he was a 'good performer', but he'd stated that he wanted to be a 'great performer'. She saw now that was her route in. If he really wanted the latter, what did he need to do to achieve that?

We spent the rest of the session talking through Paula's strategy for having this conversation with Stephen. How would she start the conversation? What exactly would she say? How would Stephen react? How would Paula then respond? By the end of the session Paula said she felt emotionally ready and prepared to have a robust conversation with Stephen. Although I held the TA framework in my head and concentrated on Adult-to-Adult conversations, I didn't actually share the model with Paula. It didn't seem necessary, and may, I felt, have been a distraction. However, it certainly helped me organise my thoughts. At the end of the session I asked Paula for some feedback. She commented that the session had been 'enlightening'. With Stephen she'd 'Felt stuck and was looking for some questions to get myself unstuck'. She said my questions had been really helpful in this context.

Why not try one of the following exercises, either for yourself or with a coaching client.

EXERCISE 1

Think about two challenging situations you've had at work, one which went well and one which didn't go so well.

What was the difference between the two? In particular, which Ego states (Parent/Adult/Child) did you/the other person adopt?

What do you need to do more of to engage in Adult-to-Adult conversations?

EXERCISE 2

This activity is similar to Exercise 1, but has a more creative bias, utilising the Persona face cards introduced in Chapter Ten.

Invite your coachee to share the essence of a challenging relationship with another person, for example 'This person really irritates me'.

Invite your coachee to choose a card that represents the other person in the relationship.

Then ask them to choose a card that represents themselves in this relationship.

Then ask, 'What other part of you do you bring?' (for example, little girl, petulant child) and find a card/cards to represent this part.

Ask your coachee what other part the challenging person brings to the relationship (for example wise old man, scary woman) and choose a card/cards to represent this part.

Now use a 'light touch' enquiry style to see what is emerging for your coachee.

- What is the difference between the cards you've chosen to represent you?
- What happens to the relationship when 'little girl' show up?
- What happens to the relationship when 'old wise man' shows up?
- Which Ego states are you/the other person adopting?
- Which part of you do you need to bring to have a more adult-to-adult discussion with this person?

Another model that I find myself referring to when I hear my coachee describing the dynamics of a relationship they are involved with and hear expressions such as 'wanting to help someone' or 'wanting to punish them' or feeling like 'I was being punished' is the Karpman Drama Triangle.

I was introduced to the Karpman Drama Triangle a number of years ago and so it was something I knew of and could describe. However, it was only when I was reintroduced to this by Miriam Orriss at the CSA that I really started to understand the model and the power of it in both coaching and supervision. The following description of the Karpman Drama Triangle and the two exercises at the end of this chapter both take their inspiration and words from Miriam and are reproduced with her kind permission.

The Karpman Drama Triangle was originally conceived by Steven Karpman as a means of describing the interplay between two or more people. Karpman's work was based on Berne's TA Model. Berne hypothesised that people form a 'Script': in essence their concept or belief of who they are, what the world is like, how they relate to the world, how the world relates to them and how others treat them. Berne believed that these 'Scripts' are created when we are very young, based on what we are told, what we experience and how we interpret these external stimuli.

At the centre of Berne's research was the theory that we all play 'Games'. A 'Game' is an unconsciously motivated behavioural interaction with the world, our environment and people with whom we are in contact. 'Games' drive our actions and behaviours to such an extent that we often find ourselves in a familiar situation, with a familiar feeling of 'here we go again'. This feeling in turn reinforces our beliefs about ourselves, the world, others. In Berne's terms, this then becomes our 'Script'.

Whilst the Karpman Drama Triangle's origins are as a therapeutic tool, it is also a useful tool to understand communication and the moves of a series of transactions between people. I use it in coaching to help people understand the roles they are in, why they are feeling the way they do and what is likely to happen next if they just let the Game take its course.

In the Karpman Drama Triangle there are three roles:

The Rescuer. A Rescuer is someone who seeks to rescue those they perceive as vulnerable. The traits of a Rescuer are that they will usually do more than half of the work and may offer 'help' unasked rather than seeking out whether the individual wants help and, if so, what form that help may take. This may mean that what the Rescuer does is not actually what the other person wanted. Ultimately this means that the Rescuer will often end up feeling resentful or unappreciated in some way. The Rescuer does not take responsibility for themselves and their own vulnerability, instead taking responsibility for the perceived Victim whom they rescue. The Rescuer will always end up feeling the Victim, but may be perceived by onlookers as the Persecutor.

The Victim. A Victim is someone who feels overwhelmed by their own sense of vulnerability or powerlessness. They do not take responsibility for themselves and therefore look for a Rescuer to look after them. At some point the Victim may feel let down by their Rescuer, or even persecuted by them. At this stage the Victim will move to the Persecutor position and persecute their former Rescuer. However, the Victim will still perceive themselves internally as the Victim.

The Persecutor. The position of Persecutor is synonymous with being unaware of one's own power and therefore discounting it. The power used is negative and often destructive. Any player in the Game may at any time be experienced as the Persecutor by the other player/players. However, the same player's internal perception may be that they are being persecuted and that they are in fact the Victim.

The three roles are depicted in figure 17.

Karpman devised a formula which plots the move of a Game. This is:

Con + Hook = Series of Complementary
Transactions → Switch → Pay Off

The moves of the Game are as follows:

Someone, usually the Victim, presents a Con – for example 'Can you help me?'

This Con matches the specific hook of the person to whom it is directed, who will usually be a Rescuer. The Rescuer responds by saying 'Yes, of course I can help you.'

The Game has now started, and will continue with a series of complementary transactions for as long as it suits both parties. At some stage one party often becomes discontented and pulls the Switch, causing the players rapidly to move positions around the triangle. At this point the Rescuer usually becomes the Victim and the Victim often becomes the Persecutor. The Game is now over and both players retire with that old familiar feeling – it's happened again.

Figure 17 The Karpman Drama Triangle

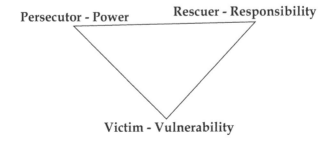

To stop the game effectively:

- The Rescuer needs to take responsibility for him/herself, acknowledge their own power and vulnerability.
- The Victim needs to own their vulnerability and take responsibility for themselves. They also need to recognise that they do have power and are able to use it appropriately.
- The Persecutor needs initially to own their power, rather than be afraid of it or use it covertly.

All very interesting and complicated, you may be thinking, but how does all this manifest itself in a coaching conversation, and how, as coaches, can we highlight the Game and encourage the coachee to end the Game somehow?

The Karpman Drama Triangle in Action

I asked Laura, a fellow coach, what she wanted to work on during our coaching session, to which she immediately replied 'Endings'.

She continued, 'Well, I've got three clients. One I did some work for years ago, one a couple of years ago and one just last year. They keep coming back for more unpaid coaching. You know, the odd catch up coffee here and there. There's one person in particular. You know, we met up for a drink last week, she was late, she dumped on me for a couple of hours, and I even ended up paying for the drinks. She sees me as a friend. But actually she knows nothing about me. I don't regard her as a friend. In fact, I don't care if I never see her again.'

I was somewhat bemused by the nature of this problem. Three clients in about ten years of coaching didn't seem to be a big problem to me. There had to be more to it than that.

'So what's *really* the issue?' I asked.

Laura stated how she wanted to fix this for the future. 'If someone comes back to me once the coaching has finished I may, at my discretion, meet with them once, but make it clear that it's not a pattern.' She paused, and then continued, 'Actually, the other two I can deal with, so it's only Jane.'

Ah…so the problem was Jane. 'If you don't care if you don't see her again, why don't you tell her what you've just told me?' I enquired.

'I couldn't, I'd feel awful. Dreadful. I just couldn't. I feel mean saying that. In the scheme of things it's not that big a deal. Three times a year…a drink, etc. It's the Rescuer in me.'

Finally, I was starting to get it. The Karpman Drama Triangle swam into my vision. Laura as the Rescuer, Jane as the Victim. Laura was now starting to feel like the Victim…The players were about to move around the board.

I looked across at Laura and noticed her physiology and posture. She'd retreated further into her chair, her shoulders hunched. As she described the issues she pointed in the shape of a circle. It was as if the players were moving around the board. Laura was spinning, not knowing what to do next, and I felt that spinning too in the pit of my stomach.

After a long pause, Laura sighed and said, 'I really don't know what it's about.'

I felt at a loss. In my own coaching I've always believed that clients have all the resources to find their own answers, they may just need a little help. Laura was an experienced coach, she knew all this stuff, but she was very obviously at a loss. I needed to take a different approach.

I took a deep breath. 'This may sound a little directive, do challenge me, but I get the sense that Jane is the embodiment of your difficulty in dealing with closure. She's walking around, inviting you to sessions; the coaching is over, so there's no contract. Jane determined the meeting place, you even paid for the drinks. It sounds as if it's all on her agenda and her terms. You're still treating her as the client.'

There was a long pause.

'Yes, you're absolutely right,' Laura replied. I noticed there was real energy and vigour in her voice now.

'What would it be like to have it more on your agenda, your terms?' I asked.

At this point Laura became completely transformed and energised. A huge smile lit up her face, she sat up. I felt a sudden shift in energy, a lightness appeared.

'Great idea. I'll respond on my terms. "I'm happy to meet you, but no free coaching this time. You dumped on me for two hours last time. This time it's my turn...and you can pay for the drinks!" Yes, I could completely do that. Best case scenario, it's fun. Worst case, she's not getting what she wants so she goes and finds it somewhere else.'

Two weeks later I received the following email from Laura.

'Thank you so much for my coaching session. I had a meeting arranged with Jane next week and I told her that I had loads I wanted to talk through with her for a change. She sent me a text yesterday saying she can't make it now – might be coincidental, but the new approach seems to be working.'

My intention, in the above scenario, had been to get Laura to recognise that she was playing a Game with Jane and to appreciate that she had choices with regard to whether or not she continued the Game. In short, to take responsibility for herself and allow Jane to take responsibility for herself, a position of equality in which the responsibility of both individuals was acknowledged.

Why not try these exercises, either for yourself or with a coaching client.

EXERCISE 1

Think of a situation where, on reflection, you have been a Rescuer, Victim or Persecutor. You may have played more than one role in the same scenario. Holding that situation in your mind, ask yourself the following questions:

- What am I doing?
- What am I not doing?
- What do I need to do?
- Who is taking responsibility for whom in this situation?
- Who am I taking responsibility for?
- Am I allowing the other person to take responsibility for themselves and their actions?
- Who has the power? How do I know?

- Have I agreed to more than I want to do?
- Am I doing more than half of the work?
- Am I owning my power positively and appropriately?
- Am I using my power to set my own boundaries and take responsibility for myself and actions?
- What boundaries do I need to set up?
- Am I using my power to take care of myself properly?
- What am I feeling about the situation? What would I like to feel?
- What action do I need to take to make sure that I deal with this in the best possible way so that it has the best possible outcome?

EXERCISE 2

Explore the Karpman Drama Triangle in relation to your coaching practice in general and in relation to your past or present coachees.

*…One cannot build on weaknesses.
To achieve results, one has to use
all of the available strengths…These
strengths are the true opportunities.*

Peter Drucker

CHAPTER TWELVE

A STRENGTHS-BASED APPROACH TO COACHING

Widely credited as being one of the first people actively to promote a strengths-based approach to development, Peter Drucker highlighted the value of focussing on someone's strengths and lamented the standard practice of companies hiring people for their skills and then subsequently identifying their weaknesses and expecting them to correct these deficiencies.

Many others have since followed in Drucker's footsteps. In 2000 Seligman and Csikszentmihalyi published what became the landmark positive psychology issue of the *American Psychologist*, stating:

> *Psychologists need to recognise that much of the best work they already do in the consulting room is to amplify strengths rather than to repair the weaknesses of their clients.*

The following year Buckingham and Clifton (2001) argued that the two most questionable but prevalent assumptions about people are 1) that each person can learn to be competent in almost anything and 2) that each person's greatest room for improvement is in their area of greatest weakness. More recently Zenger and Folkman (2009) have continued this theme:

> *One of the basic questions facing everyone creating a personal development plan is the fundamental question*

of whether to focus attention on correcting faults and failings or whether to focus on building strengths. Like many questions that appear simple, there are some interesting complexities.

Zenger and Folkman argue that people naturally gravitate towards their weaknesses. There is some kind of tacit assumption that our strengths come from unseen sources and will take care of themselves. 'Real development' is about discovering what we are bad at and working on that.

Likewise, in the coaching context, as coaches we are more likely to be contracted to help fix weakness, because weakness is believed to result in risk and cost. At a chemistry session I rarely find a coachee talking about their strengths and how they want to build on these. Instead they will talk about 'weaknesses' or 'development needs' and making these the focus of our coaching sessions. Indeed, organisationally employees are continually encouraged to focus on and address their weaknesses – a message that is often reinforced via HR processes such as performance appraisal, competency frameworks and pay-reward schemes. In general individuals are not encouraged to develop and capitalise on their strengths and what they do best.

However, this is not necessarily true outside of the organisational context. In sport there is an established practice of 'playing to your strengths'. When David Beckham retired from playing football, sports writers filled newspaper pages analysing the footballing ability of a player who was generally accepted as the star player in a golden generation. The verdict? He was not gifted with the greatest of speed and could not tackle, but he had an amazing ability to cross the ball with his right foot. In short, Beckham had successfully built his football career around a key strength, honed through years of practice on Manchester United's training pitch. Similarly Jessica Ennis won the heptathlon gold medal in the London 2012 Olympics Games despite being slight of build and almost a foot shorter than some of her rivals. She had successfully built her profile as a heptathlete around her unmatched sprinting ability and honed her technique in her 'weaker' events to play to her strengths.

'But does taking a strengths-based approach actually work?' I hear you ask. Evidence appears to suggest that it does. In a study of 19,187 employees from thirty-four organisations across seven industries and twenty-nine counties, the Corporate Leadership Council (2002) found that when managers emphasised performance strengths, performance in these strengths was 36.4% higher. In contrast, emphasising weaknesses led to a 26.8% decline in these weaknesses. Zenger and Folkman noticed similar results in a study of leaders in a packaged food company group. Those that focused on weakness made an improvement of 12%. However, those that worked on a combination of strengths and weaknesses improved by 36%. A wealth of other studies exists linking the use of strengths to higher levels of energy and vitality, reduced stress, increased resilience, higher self-esteem, achievement of goals and happiness.

All of which, I believe, raises some potentially interesting questions for us as coaches. Should we be telling our coachees to forget about their weaknesses or areas for development and simply concentrate on building their strengths? I would argue that it really depends on the nature of our weaknesses. If my coachee possesses a profound career-limiting weakness – for example, in his new role he needs to manage budgets and put monthly financial data together and his finance and IT skills are poor – then he needs to work on these. Working on strengths is relatively futile until these fundamental weaknesses are rectified. I often use the analogy of a boat. My strengths are my sail and my weaknesses are the hole in the boat. With the benefit of a large sail, a small hole can be compensated for. But if the hole is too big and the sail too small that boat will sink.

What Zenger and Folkman refer to as 'fatal flaws' do need to be addressed. After that, encouraging our coachees to 'play to their strengths' as a way of unlocking their potential can be a highly effective way of coaching.

There are a number of tools to help coaches identify their strengths, including:

The Clifton Strengths Finder. Based on more than thirty years of research, this tool was developed by Donald Clifton and his colleagues at the Gallup Organisation. The questionnaire assesses thirty-four themes of talent, primarily within applied occupational settings, and provides a feedback report that documents the respondent's top five themes of talent.

The VIA classification of strengths. Developed by Christopher Peterson and Martin Seligman, the VIA was one of the early initiatives of the positive psychology movement. The questionnaire measures twenty-four 'signature strengths', loosely organised under six virtues (wisdom and knowledge, courage, humanity, justice, temperance and transcendence). Respondents are provided with a feedback report with a brief description of their five 'signature strengths'. A signature strength is something that conveys a sense of ownership and authenticity – a sense of 'this is the real me'. Peterson and Seligman argue that we all have a sense of yearning to act in accordance with our strengths. There is a powerful intrinsic motivation to use the strength.

R2 Strengths Profiler. Developed by Capp, the R2 Strengths Profiler is a strengths assessment and development tool. The R2 Strengths Profiler assesses sixty strengths according to three dimensions of energy, performance and use.

In my own coaching practice I tend to use the R2 Strengths Profiler tool. Capp's definition of a strength resonates with me:

A natural capacity for behaving, thinking or feeling in a way that allows optimal functioning and performance in the pursuit of valued outcomes.

(LINLEY AND HARRINGTON, 2006)

Likewise I find that coachees connect with the three dimensions of energy, performance and use when thinking about their work, and find the language of the questionnaire straightforward and easy to relate to. I will therefore focus on using the R2 Strengths Profiler as a way of working with strengths during this chapter, whilst recognising that there are other tools that some may prefer to use.

When introducing coachees to the concept of strengths and weaknesses, be it individually or as part of a training programme, I ask them first of all to speak about something that drains them; that they are no good at. After a few minutes I then ask them to switch to something they are good at and that energises them and talk about that. I then share observations – what people saw and heard either as the speaker or the listener.

People invariably use the following types of expressions to describe talking about weaknesses:

- Their tone was monotone with little 'colour'
- The energy level felt low and there were few gestures
- The speaker sat slumped in their chair
- The speaker didn't appear to be themselves
- As the listener it was hard to visualise what they were telling you

Conversely, when speakers switch to talking about something they are good at and energises them, the following descriptions are common:

- There is an immediate switch in tone – like switching from a minor to major key
- The atmosphere is relaxed, but focused and energised
- The speaker uses phrases like 'I love it' and 'it's really me'
- There is a sense of their descriptions being authentic and integrated. They may even tell you they've always loved doing this, even as a child.
- As they speak, the speaker is passionate and absorbed in their subject. For the listener it is easy to visualise as the descriptions are detailed and vivid

As a coach there are several ways that we can use a strengths based approach in our coaching practice. The first is listening out for strengths in order to identify and harness coachee's strengths. Practically as a coach this means being really present in coaching sessions. In Linley's (2006) words, wearing 'strengths-tinted lenses' and being:

A keen observer of the ebb and flow of the coaching conversation, being finely attuned to the subtle nuances of language and emotion that might indicate the presence of a strength.

We can then reflect our observations back to our coachee as a way of working with them to identify strengths. For example, 'I noticed when you talked about x there was a real shift in your energy: you suddenly sat really upright, your tone changed – you spoke faster, there was more "colour" in your voice. I noticed you used the words "love doing", "feel energised", "I'm good at". I haven't heard you using these expressions before. I am wondering if you noticed a change in yourself... and what that might mean.'

We can then help to raise the strength within the coachee's consciousness with a view to further exploring, developing and seeking opportunities to apply this strength in the future.

The following is an example of a strengths based approach to a coaching conversation.

Strengths based coaching questions

- What are the things that you do best?
- How do you know when you are at your best?
- What are the key strengths and resources that you can build upon to find a solution to this situation?
- Tell me about a time when you were successful at doing this before.

- Tell me about a time when you learned something quickly. How did you do it?
- Who do you know who has done this successfully? How did they do it?
- What do you feel is the answer that is coming from inside you?
- What were you really good at as a child? How can you apply some of that x to this situation?
- What strength/skill would you really love to use at work? How could you use that in this situation?

These are questions we can ask at any time – we do not need our coachee to have taken any strengths-based questionnaire. However, if I feel a coachee is really struggling to identify their strengths or would benefit from a deeper understanding of their strengths and weaknesses I will suggest that they take the R2 Strengths Profiler.

The R2 Strengths Profiler analyses sixty strengths from five strengths families:

- Being – our way of being
- Communicating – how we communicate
- Motivating – drivers for action
- Relating – how we relate
- Thinking – what we focus on

The questionnaire generates a profile comprising of up to seven realised strengths, seven unrealised strengths, four learned behaviours and three weaknesses. This terminology is explained below.

Realised strengths are the strengths we have and know we have. They energise us, we deploy them to good effect and we use them frequently.

Unrealised strengths are the strengths we have but maybe do not appreciate fully yet. They energise us, we deploy them to good effect, but they remain in the background waiting for the opportunity to be used and developed more fully.

Learned behaviours are the attributes that we use effectively, but they do not energise us. Learned behaviours are often misinterpreted as strengths.

Weaknesses are the attributes where we are not effective. Our weaknesses do not energise us and we may or may not be aware of them. We are likely to be using some of our weaknesses to the extent that they may be causing us concern or problems. Other weaknesses are less likely to be of relevance to our situation.

Having identified your strengths and weaknesses, the R2 Strengths Profiler then promotes the 4M Model for development.

Marshal our realised strengths. Think about situations where we can use our strengths more (or less if we over-rely on them). Think about which strengths we can use together to best effect.

Maximise our unrealised strengths. Find opportunities to use these, to practise them, to extend and expand our reach.

Moderate our learned behaviours. Stop doing it or do less of it. Consider whether you need to let anyone else know that you want to do less of this – as we are good at doing these things we tend to attract more of them. Find a complementary partner – someone who enjoys and is good at this.

Minimise our weaknesses. Aim to have less recourse to them until they are no longer a problem. Use strengths to compensate. Undertake training/development to become as good as you need to be.

During a coaching session I will use the 4M Model to encourage the coachee to think about how they can marshal and maximise their strengths, moderate their learned behaviours and minimise their weaknesses. Here are some useful prompt questions, adapted from Capp's R2 Strengths Profiler, to facilitate this process.

COACHING SCENARIO – WORKING ON MY WEAKNESSES

The following are useful prompt questions when a coachee says they want to work on their weaknesses. 'Want' may mean that they genuinely want to, that this weakness is now a potential flaw and they need to address it and/or they have been given specific feedback that they need to address it.

Is this issue a potential 'fatal flaw' or business critical?

How is the issue affecting you? What is the impact on performance? How do you feel about the situation?

- Where are you now on a scale of 1 to 10?
- Where would you like to be on a scale of 1 to 10? Over what timeframe?
- What would an improvement look like/feel like?
- What have you tried so far that has worked?
- What will you commit to doing? When? How?
- How will you know you have been successful?

As a coach:

- What do you notice about their energy? Affirm what you see working.

226

- What themes and ideas are you hearing? Play these back.
- What insight can you offer?

COACHING SCENARIO – WORKING ON MY UNREALISED STRENGTHS

The following are useful prompt questions when a coachee wants to work on their unrealised strengths, but doesn't know yet how they can use these strengths more.

- Where's the big opportunity?
- How can you find a way to use this strength more? What options do you have? What else…? What if…?
- Who do you know who has this strength and uses it well?
- If you could be using this strength more, what would that look like/feel like?
- Where would you say you are now on a scale of 1 to 10? What are the reasons for your score?
- What would it look like/feel like if you moved up a notch?
- In your role, what opportunities are there for increasing the frequency of use? What opportunities can you create? How can you stretch yourself more?
- Is there a learned behaviour you could replace with an unrealised strength?
- What do you get from using this learned behaviour? What is the outcome?
- What could you do to get the same outcome but be more energised in the process?
- What would it be like if you swapped x out and swapped y in?
- What will you do to make this happen?

FOOD FOR THOUGHT
MAXIMISING YOUR STRENGTHS

Maximise your strengths by changing the way you think. Start shifting your own perspective by putting the tips below into practice:

- Write your own story/personal brand. We choose the story that we tell other people about ourselves. Understanding our strengths and being able to talk to others about them can enable us to let others know who we are.

- Understand how your realised strengths play out in your life for the best. How do you use them? When do you use them? With whom do you use them? How have they positively influenced your life as it is today? Start to use your realised strengths consciously every day.

- Get feedback. Ask someone who knows you well to choose your top strengths for you. Ask them to give you specific examples of the strengths in action.

- Adjust the volume dial. Take control and consider which strengths are best used in each situation. As you become more aware you can learn to use your strengths, decreasing the volume in one area as you draw upon strengths in other areas.

- Use strengths to overcome weaknesses. When stuck in a situation where you are depending on your weaknesses too much – stop and think. How can you use a strength, or combination of strengths, to achieve your goal instead?

- Use your strengths in a novel way. Strengthen their effect in your life by extending their reach. So, for instance, if 'curiosity' is one of your strengths and you use it currently when faced with a problem, try visiting an art gallery or research a new subject.
- Manage your energy. When you know that you have a potentially draining day coming up, think about how you can start and finish the day with things that energise you.
- Find a complementary partner. Seek out people who can compensate for your weakness, and vice versa.
- 'To do' lists. Notice the things that never make it on to your 'to do' list. The things that always seem to get done often reveal an underlying strength which means we never need to be asked twice.

STRENGTHS IN ACTION

I was just starting work with a new coachee, James. During our first session James explained how he'd been with his organisation for a number of years. He was internally recognised as a high performer and his career to date had seen a number of promotions and moves to different sites. He had been in his current role for approximately eighteen months, and both he and the site had performed well. However, he was aware that his role was about to change. The site he managed was undergoing a major expansion. This expansion included a factory expansion as well as new products and state of the art machinery which required different skill sets and ways of working. In addition, James was about to reorganise his leadership team, which would include some current members leaving the leadership team as well as recruiting some new key players, most probably from outside the organisation. James wanted the coaching to focus on preparing him for this role. He admitted that he was struggling to see himself in the future responsible for this huge site. He knew he needed to be different, but he wasn't quite sure what needed to change.

James had previously done some reading on playing to your strengths and was interested in adopting a strengths-based approach to his own development. I therefore invited him to complete the R2 Strengths Profiler and suggested that we use this as a framework for our next meeting. James was keen to follow this approach.

We started by exploring James's realised strengths and how suited these were for this new, bigger role. I used the analogy of the volume control on a radio. Were there any strengths that he was using too much/over-relying on (i.e. the volume control was set too high)? James immediately pointed to 'Personal Responsibility', his number one strength. He commented that he took great pride in delivering on personal commitments, taking ownership and not blaming others. However, he recognised that this meant that he sometimes took on too much himself and didn't delegate authority and responsibility to others. He recognised that he needed to tone down this strength, delegate more to his team and hold others accountable, especially as his role would be getting even bigger.

When it came to exploring weaknesses, James recognised that 'Listener' and 'Relationship Deepener' were areas where he struggled. He acknowledged that he tended to be more task than people focused. He also acknowledged that he had received feedback, directly from team members and during his last performance appraisal, that this was an area that he needed to work on. James believed that he wasn't as good at these as he needed to be and identified these as areas that he would like to work on during our coaching.

Our richest discussions were saved for exploring James's unrealised strengths. James picked out 'Strategic Awareness', 'Reconfiguration' and 'Catalyst' as things that he enjoyed doing, gave him energy and he'd used successfully in previous roles. He recognised that he'd become too task and detail focussed in his current role, partly due to some gaps in his leadership team and a need for him to plug them. However, he needed to move away from this detail and short term focus and adopt a more strategic focus for his new role.

By the end of the session we'd identified what skills, behaviours and knowledge James needed for his new role, and James had drawn up his own personal SWOT in relation to this role. James had also identified the priority areas to work on, and these then became the focus of our coaching sessions.

In summary, working with strengths is a different space to be working in as a coach – all too often coachees present their 'weaknesses' as areas to work on. However, it can be a hugely enjoyable and enlightening space to focus on for coachees, and, if it's an area that you've not explored, I would encourage you to have a go.

*Between stimulus and response
there is a space.
In that space is the power to choose
our response.
In our response lies our growth and
freedom.*

Viktor Frankl

CHAPTER THIRTEEN

SELF MANAGEMENT

'I've got an example' We all turned our attention to Andrew. He'd been fairly quiet in the workshops so far, and it was unusual for him to speak up in front of the whole group.

'Well I'd had a really busy day at work,' he continued. 'Everything seemed to be going wrong, and on the way home I stopped off at the supermarket. The car park was really busy and I'd just spotted a free space and was about to drive into it when this woman appeared from nowhere and nicked my spot. I was furious! I sounded my horn and shouted at her. I then parked somewhere else and marched over and gave her a piece of my mind. I don't know what came over me. I suppose it was the last straw. I couldn't believe it afterwards. I was just so ashamed of my behaviour. My three-year-old would have behaved better.'

So what happened to Andrew? What made him switch from a mild-mannered rational adult to a three-year-old having a tantrum in the supermarket car park? As discussed at the start of Chapter Eleven, Daniel Goleman argues that there are four tenets of emotional intelligence: self-awareness, self-management, social awareness and relationship management. In simple terms what Andrew experienced was a loss of self-control. To understand the above transformation in Andrew we first need to understand the human brain and how it works.

The human brain has three parts to it:

- The reptilian brain. This is the oldest part of the brain and sits above the spinal cord. This part houses control centres that prompt breathing, swallowing and heart beating. As long as the reptilian brain survives it will keep the heart beating, the lungs expanding and relaxing and salt and water balanced in the blood.

- The limbic brain. 'Limbic' is from the Latin word *limbus*, meaning 'edge, margin or border', so called because this structure marks the evolutionary division between two disparate ways of life. This brain drapes itself around the reptilian brain. Mammals have this brain, but reptiles do not. The amygdala is an almond shaped mass of nuclei located deep within the limbic part of the brain and is involved in many of our emotions and motivations, particularly those related to survival. The amygdala is also responsible for determining what memories are stored in the brain. It is thought that this determination is based on how huge an emotional response an event evokes.

- The neocortex, from the Greek for 'new' and the Latin for 'rind' or 'bark', is the final part of the brain and, in humans, the largest of the three brains. Speaking, writing, planning and reasoning all originate in the neocortex. So do the experiences of our senses, what we know as 'awareness', and our conscious motor control, what we know as 'will'. The neocortex bestows us with the skill of abstraction – language being the most impressive and perhaps the most useful abstraction we have.

When we are operating under normal conditions, stimuli come in from our eyes and ears and go to the thalamus, before part of the signal goes directly to the amygdala and part to the thinking part (neocortex). The thalamus acts as an air traffic controller to keep the signals moving. Normally action is taken based on input from both areas, the amygdala and the neocortex.

However, when we perceive a crisis our brains are designed to help us short-cut this effective but slow process. Like any skilled air traffic controller, the thalamus can quickly react to a potential threat. Therefore in perceived emergencies the thalamus bypasses the neocortex, the thinking brain, and the signal goes straight to the amygdala. The power of emotion overwhelms rationality. In such cases the amygdala can only react based on its limited number of stored patterns. Daniel Goleman coined a phrase for this response – an 'Amygdala Hijack'.

The above operation works well in true crises when speed of action is important, for example 'fight' or 'flight' responses. However, genuine fight or flight responses are not called for much in today's world, so what gets interpreted as a crisis is more often a conflict in a work setting, or an unpleasant encounter with a family member, or, in the case of Andrew, with a stranger in a supermarket car park. In these cases a visceral emotional reaction is probably not appropriate or effective.

According to Daniel Goleman, an Amygdala Hijack has three distinct components:

- A strong emotional reaction to the situation (e.g. anger, desire, fear, frustration)
- An instant, impulsive, irrational or uncontrolled reaction that is usually inappropriate

- A subsequent feeling of regret or remorse after the strong emotions pass and there has been some opportunity for reflection.

If I am explaining an Amygdala Hijack to an individual or group, at this point I usually ask if they can think of any high profile Amygdala Hijacks. The following infamous incident is invariably mentioned.

This is when Zinedine Zidane lost his self-control and head-butted Marco Materazzi in the 2006 World Cup final. Zidane was sent off and France subsequently lost the World Cup to Italy. Zidane retired immediately after the game with his career ending in disgrace. The 28.8 million viewers in 213 countries were all left wondering what on earth Zidane was thinking. Why did he ruin his reputation by acting so stupidly? But, of course, Zidane wasn't thinking. His logical reasoning had been hijacked by the powerful survival reaction of the amygdala. Zidane later apologised for setting a bad example to children. However, he remained unrepentant to Materazzi, rationalising that Materazzi had provoked him.

'All very interesting, but what is the relevance of all of this to coaching?' you may be asking. I think it is of paramount importance. Many organisations today are full of people walking around with stress and concerns about the future. Equally, advances in technology mean that we are essentially contactable 24/7. The majority of the people I coach work long hours in the office and often continue to pick up emails and phone messages at home. Continually working under such intense pressure makes us more vulnerable to

Amygdala Hijacks. Indeed, research by Hay Group has shown that we are more likely to have Amygdala Hijacks when:

- We are feeling tired
- We have a build-up of stressors – the 'last straw' syndrome
- We have invested significant effort into something
- We have been drinking alcohol
- We are involved in an activity closely related to our motivations

Research has also shown that emotions are contagious. So if one person on the team is emotionally hijacked, other people may catch it, resulting in teamwork and collaboration deteriorating. The leader's ability to manage their emotions is therefore paramount as they are effectively the emotional thermostat for their team and can significantly influence the team's mood and productivity. Research by Hay Group found that the leader has 50–70% influence over the climate of the team.

If I am exploring self-management issues with my coachee, my focus is on:

- Firstly heightening their self-awareness and understanding that he/she has been acting differently. For example, losing their temper more frequently or suddenly getting tearful in meetings.
- Secondly enabling them to gain an understanding of why this might be. What factors are triggering these responses?

Having spent some time reflecting on the first and second points, we concentrate on learning some new strategies for adopting different and more appropriate responses.

I invariably invite my coachee to complete the following activity, exploring a recent situation when they felt they could have handled things better.

EXERCISE – SELF MANAGEMENT IN ACTION

Think of a recent situation when, on reflection, you could have handled things better. A situation that left you feeling some regret or remorse about the approach you took. A sense of 'I could have handled that better'. Consider the following questions and make some notes in response to each one:

- Could I have changed the situation? In hindsight, could I have seen it coming? Could I have avoided putting myself in the situation in the first place?
- Could I have changed how I viewed the situation? Could I have chosen a different perspective? Could I have taken a more positive view of the situation?
- What could I have done to change my reaction to the situation? Was I aware of the strength of my feelings? Could I name what those feelings were? Did I anticipate the impact of my feelings on myself and others?

The above activity invariably prompts some interesting reflection, particularly in relation to how much choice the coachee actually had in the situation.

Having identified what causes us to have an Amygdala Hijack, the next stage is to develop some strategies to avoid it happening in future. The key to this is in sharpening our radar, i.e. practising ways of monitoring our feelings while they are still suitable and before the intensity builds up. This is demonstrated in figure 18.

238

Figure 18 Avoiding an Amygdala Hijack

Heighten your awareness: Monitor your feelings before they build in strength

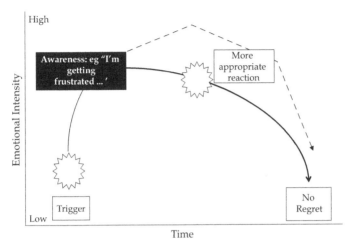

In summary, there are four key steps to managing our amygdala:

- Knowing our triggers – what pushes our button?
- Identifying our chain of responses – what happens first, second, etc.?
- Identifying our self-talk – what do we start to tell ourselves?
- Challenging our self-talk – what would be more useful to tell ourselves?

This is explained in more detail below.

KNOWING OUR TRIGGERS

In seeking to avoid Amygdala Hijacks, we first need to know what is likely to cause us to have one in the first place. A useful way of understanding what our key triggers are is by looking back at past hijacks – what was our motivation and what form of hijack was the result? For example:

- A need to achieve may result in us inappropriately taking a task from someone rather than taking the time to coach them how to complete it.
- A need to be in control may result in a reluctance to delegate tasks, and then having an angry outburst because we are overloaded.
- A need for recognition may result in extreme anger at perceived threats to status.

IDENTIFYING YOUR CHAIN OF RESPONSES

The next stage is to identify the physical and mental chain of reactions that you find yourself experiencing in these situations. Think back to a hijack situation and put yourself back into that time right now. As you start to relive this situation, what do you notice about yourself? For example, a sinking feeling, a sense of anger rising from the pit of my stomach, butterflies in my stomach, hands sweating, my heart starting to race, thinking that I want to run out of the room…

Notice the order in which you experience these emotions/ sensations. What happens first? What happens next?

IDENTIFYING YOUR SELF-TALK

Having identified that you are experiencing a strong emotion, you then need to understand what is leading you to experience that emotion. Essentially it is our perceptions of situations that determine our emotional responses. Several people in a room may actually experience the same situation and yet individual perceptions of it may be quite different. We therefore need to identify what we are saying to ourselves about the situation we are in. Here our knowledge of our common trigger situations and our common motivations can give us some clues. Some useful questions to ask ourselves to identify our self-talk are:

- 'What does this situation mean to me?' (This could include personal values/beliefs/ motivations that are being challenged.)
- 'What is it about this situation that is leading me to feel this way?'

CHALLENGING YOUR SELF-TALK

Once we have identified the thoughts that are underpinning our emotions, we can then work at changing them, including a conscious choice to tell ourselves something different.

HANDLING MY AMYGDALA – IN ACTION

One of my coachees, Sue, had identified regulating her emotions as one of her outcomes for our coaching. At one of our sessions she described how she had recently returned from a very important meeting overseas. All of her peers were there, as well as her boss and her counterpart. Sue described how, from her perspective, the meeting had not gone well. One of her peers had dominated discussions in the afternoon session and had repeatedly talked over Sue. She had felt quite emotional in the second part of the meeting and had effectively withdrawn from it. She described how, on the way back to the airport, she had shared her experience of the meeting with a colleague. Whilst the colleague had similarly agreed that it hadn't been a productive meeting, he didn't appear to have been wrapped up in the emotion of it to the same extent as Sue. In fact, he actually appeared to be amused by some of the behaviours he had witnessed in the meeting. Sue was curious to understand what had gone on for her and also to develop some strategies for avoiding becoming so emotionally involved in the future.

I talked Sue through the various parts of the brain and their functions and then invited her to unpack her experience with me.

Know your triggers. Sue identified a need for recognition – she had been with the company for many years, was very experienced and believed she had a lot of knowledge to share. She also identified a need to belong. It was important for her to feel part of a team and an equal. She recognised a tendency to withdraw when she did not feel valued and part of the team.

Identifying your chain of responses. Sue identified her heart racing, a mounting sense of irritation, a desire to shout 'Shut up', followed by a desire to get out of the room and then a sense of being about to burst into tears.

Identifying your self-talk. This was the real breakthrough step for Sue as she immediately identified that she started to tell herself that this particular peer did not respect her and her opinion – otherwise she wouldn't have kept interrupting her and would have wanted to hear her views. This violated her need for recognition and need for belonging.

Challenging your self-talk. I invited Sue to change her self-talk in similar future situations. Sue recalled how, on the way back to the airport, her colleague had dismissed her concerns that this peer 'Constantly talked over me and doesn't value my opinion' with the comment 'Oh, she does that with everyone, it's not just you'. Upon reflection, Sue appreciated that her colleague was, in fact, correct. It wasn't just her, but she was choosing to focus on it being her. For Sue, adopting a different self-talk, for example: 'She's interrupting everyone, not just me, and this is being driven by her insecurity and need to be recognised' completely altered her perspective on the situation. She had now developed a new strategy which she could adopt the next time a similar situation arose.

Another tool that can help with both self-awareness and self-management is the 'Emotional Audit'. This is designed to ask questions that can change the focus when a person is emotionally charged or about to get hijacked. I suggest that coachees take a pause, metaphorically speaking counting to ten, but use this time to ask the following questions to better direct their brain's thinking.

THE EMOTIONAL AUDIT EXERCISE

This audit is helpful, especially if you are feeling 'triggered' by someone or something. Wait five seconds until you get an answer to each question. To build your self-awareness and self-management, use the audit several times a day. As you do so you will notice patterns – what triggers you, how you are feeling and how you get in your way.

What am I thinking? This question accesses our thoughts. Generally I find most people can answer this quite quickly and tell you what they're thinking about something.

What am I feeling? This question accesses our emotions and can be trickier to answer than what we're thinking. Emotions are humanity's motivator and its omnipresent guide. Greed and ambition run beneath the surface of economics; vengefulness and reverence under the veneer of justice. There are differing views on the number of core emotions that rule our lives and what these are, but the following are generally cited: anger, fear, shame, guilt, sadness, gladness and hurt. For many people, being able to name the emotion they are feeling accurately is a real challenge. Ultimately the aim is name it to tame it.

What do I want now? This question makes conscious our intentions. What do we want to happen?

How am I getting in my way? This evaluates our actions in line with our intentions. Patterns of how we get in our way may emerge. It enables reflection and learning from mistakes.

What do I need to do differently now? This last question takes in all this new conscious data and allows us to direct our brain and actions better for the goals we want.

If Sue had built an emotional audit, this could have revealed:

- What am I thinking? What is she doing? Why is she constantly interrupting me and talking over me? She doesn't respect my opinion.
- What am I feeling? Frustrated with her and rising anger. She's not the only one with ideas, and I've got something really important to say. Possibly also a little afraid. Worried that my expertise and views are not seen as important.
- What do I want? Some uninterrupted space to say what I want/need to say. I want to be listened to.
- How am I getting in the way? I am fuming and not calming myself down. I'm starting to withdraw from the situation and just let them get on with it.

- What do I need to do differently? I need to take a breath. I need to say what I want to say assertively and succinctly. I need to challenge X's behaviour and state that I want to say what I need to say without being interrupted.

In contrast to some of the creative and light touch coaching approaches we've explored in previous chapters, this chapter has focussed on a more rational approach including mapping processes and then challenging and reframing responses. When I've adopted this approach with coachees I've found that it has invariably resulted in moments of enlightenment. A sense of 'Oh that's what happened then' and relief that 'It's not just me then … this is normal'. Coachees have found exploring their chains of reaction and then challenging these both insightful and empowering as they decide to consciously choose an alternative response.

The soul is dyed the colour of its thoughts. Think only those things that are in line with your principles and can bear the light of day. The content of your character is your choice. Day by day, what you do is who you become. Your integrity is your destiny – it is the light that guides your way.

Heraclitus

CHAPTER FOURTEEN

DEVELOPING A LEADERSHIP STYLE

When discussing potential coaching outcomes with managerial level coachees, the word 'leadership' invariably comes up. Perhaps the coachee has recently had a promotion and now has a bigger team with more direct reports, and is conscious that they need to be less 'hands on' and delegate more to others. Maybe they have received feedback that their current style is too 'this' or 'that' and they are hoping that coaching will enable them to develop a more rounded leadership style. Or maybe they are just aware that what they are doing currently isn't working – they are working too many hours, doing too much themselves, having challenging relationships with members of their team – and they need to do something different. The trouble is they are not sure what.

Having identified that the coachee wants to work on their leadership style, I ask them to describe their current leadership style. Whilst they can obviously do this in words, I often invite coachees to choose photographs to do so. As already described in Chapter Ten, using creative approaches can be incredibly useful in enabling coaching clients to gain insight into the dynamics of the situation they are caught up in. I invite my coachee to select a number of photographs – at least one that says something about their current leadership style and at least one that reflects how they would like their leadership style to be in six months' time, i.e. when the coaching has finished or in the coachee's chosen timeframe. Tom chose the following photographs:

- Three to describe his current leadership style. For him the giraffe represented his 'fear of putting my head above the parapet' and the rhino 'all the things that seem to be stopping me'. The woman peering into the hole represented his eagerness to learn and 'why I'm here'.
- The three on the left to represent the leadership style he aspired to in six months. The man in the sand depicting, the man in the sand depicting

Figure 19 Examples of my leadership style activity

a 'more relaxed me' and the paints 'I've now developed my own unique leadership style, I've mixed my own paints'. He saw the bird as being him 'now taking a more strategic perspective Instead of getting involved in all of the detail'.

In just a few minutes we'd started to draw out and explore some of Tom's outcomes for his coaching sessions.

'Leadership' and 'management' are terms that are often used interchangeably. During the course of a conversation, a coachee may state that they 'want to be a better manager' or that they 'need to provide more leadership', and it is not really clear if they are regarding 'management' and 'leadership' as being the same or different activities. Exploring the coachee's own perception of what these terms mean to them can therefore be a useful starting point. You can do this by asking your coachee to describe what each term means to them. Alternatively you could do the exercise described below.

ACTIVITY. LEADERSHIP VERSUS MANAGEMENT

Give your coachee the list of characteristics detailed in table 2 below and ask them to identify whether each statement applies mainly to leadership or management or equally to both leadership and management. I have found that the easiest way to complete the exercise is to transfer the statements to cards. The coachee then sorts the cards into two, or possibly three, columns, ending up with their own leadership/management identikit.

Whilst there is no definitive answer to the above activity, I believe there are enough well researched and generally agreed upon characteristics of leadership and management to make some clear distinctions.

Table 2 Leadership versus management

LEADERSHIP OR MANAGEMENT?	
Inspires a shared vision	Inspires trust
Asks 'how' and 'when'	Builds collaboration and teamwork
Focuses on performance and standards	Provides purpose and meaning
Enables others	Implements and maintains
Adopts a short-term view	Acts courageously
Engages hearts and minds	Dependable. Follows through on tasks
Achieves tasks through others	Searches for opportunities to change and improve
Establishes structures and systems	Completes transactions/ tasks
Asks 'what' and 'why'	Focuses on doing things right
Challenges the process	Plans and organises to solve problems
Focuses on people and systems running smoothly	Monitors results and plans
Provides stability and supports the status quo	Forward looking. Visionary
Strengthens the abilities of others to excel	Focuses on doing the right thing
Brings order and co-ordination	Acts authentically
Aligns and mobilises others	
Recognises the achievement of others	

As a starting point I particularly like Kouzes and Posner's (2002) definition of leadership:

Leadership is a reciprocal relationship between those who choose to lead and those who decide to follow.

For me this introduces two clear arguments in support of leadership:

- To be a true leader you need to have followers. People need to be motivated and inspired to follow you.
- Leadership can happen at various levels in an organisation, it is not exclusive to one position or level in an organisation.

Kotter (1996) makes some useful distinctions between management and leadership.

Management is a set of processes designed to keep a complicated system of people and technology running smoothly.

Leadership is a set of processes that creates organisations in the first place or adapts them to significantly changing circumstances.

Using this and other research, it is possible to make the following broad distinctions.

Management is about:

- Planning and budgeting – steps, timetables and allocating resources
- Organising and staffing – structure, delegating responsibility and authority, policies, procedures and systems

- Controlling and problem solving – monitoring results, planning and organising to solve problems
- Producing a degree of predictability and order with the potential to produce the short-term results expected by stakeholders consistently.

Leadership is about:

- Establishing direction – vision of future, strategies for change
- Aligning people – communicating by words and deeds to create teams and coalitions to support each other
- Motivating and inspiring – energising people to overcome barriers by satisfying basic, often unfulfilled, human needs
- Producing change, often dramatic, with the potential to produce extremely useful change (e.g. new products, better customer focus).

Based on the above definitions I would suggest the following possible 'answer' in table 3 to the leadership identikit exercise explained above.

The point of the activity is not for coachees to reach the 'correct' answer, but to get them thinking about how they are defining management and leadership and, as part of the process, how their current style matches up to these definitions. Coachees' definitions will be shaped by a variety of sources, including their cultural background, their own experiences of being led, whom they admire as leaders (either from first-hand experience or from their public persona), the type of organisation they work for and what is valued and the size/level of maturity of their organisation.

Table 3 Leadership versus management. One possible 'answer'

A POSSIBLE ANSWER ...	
Leadership	Management
Inspires a shared vision	Implements and maintains
Inspires trust	Dependable. Follows through on tasks
Builds collaboration and teamwork	Completes transactions/ tasks
Acts courageously	Focuses on doing things right
Searches for opportunities to change and improve	Plans and organises to solve problems
Forward looking. Visionary	Monitors results and plans
Enables others	Acts 'how' and 'when'
Engages hearts and minds	Focuses on performance and standards
Asks 'what' and 'why'	Adopts a short-term view
Challenges the process	Achieves tasks through others
Strengthens the abilities of others to excel	Establishes structures and systems
Recognises the achievement of others	Provides stability and supports the status quo
Focuses on doing the right thing	Brings order and co-ordination
Acts authentically	Focuses on people and systems running smoothly
Aligns and mobilises others	
Provides purpose and meaning	

As a next step I often invite coachees to plot their current style using a simple matrix with 'management' on one axis and 'leadership' on the other. Once they have done this, I then invite them to plot other people in their organisation.

At face value this is a very simple exercise, and yet the output never ceases to amaze me in terms of the insights it provides. For example, is the coachee providing strong management to their team but not focussing enough on articulating the longer term vision and direction? Conversely, are they spending too much time focussing on selling the vision, getting team members on board, engaging hearts and minds and not getting enough of the basics right? Equally, what kind of leadership are they experiencing? What is the dominant style of the organisation? This simple exercise can then develop into a coaching session focussing on the coachee's leadership style.

- What is going well?
- What do they need to pay attention to moving forward?
- What do they need to do more/less of?
- What do they need to start/stop/continue doing?
- How will they know they have been successful in adapting their style?

The previous two activities are useful as a means of helping a coachee gain a quick insight into leadership and their current style. If there is the need to do a more in-depth session I will often use a leadership styles framework as a basis for discussion. My preferred framework is based on the original work of Litwin and Stringer at Harvard in the 1960s. Litwin and Stringer identified six leadership styles: coercive, authoritative, democratic, pace setters, coaching and affiliative. This framework was subsequently developed and popularised by Daniel Goleman and a team of research colleagues from Hay/McBer exploring links between leadership and emotional intelligence and climate and performance. Hay Group has subsequently renamed three of the leadership styles, with 'coercive' becoming 'directive', 'authoritative' becoming 'visionary' and 'democratic' becoming 'participative'.

Prior to the arranged coaching session I will send the coachee an email inviting them to complete the following activity as pre-work and bring their notes along to the session.

LEADERSHIP STYLES EXERCISE

SITUATION 1

Identify a personal leadership situation where, due to your own efforts, you were pleased with the outcome you achieved.

(NB: this could be a situation where you were the actual leader, i.e. the manager, or a more temporary leadership role, e.g. a project management role or where, due to particular circumstances, you assumed a leadership role.)

Recall the events and make some notes to share with your coach.

Consider:

- What was the context?
- Who was involved?
- What were the events leading to the situation?
- What happened? Recall what you (and others) thought, said and did

- How did you feel? (Consider both during and after)
- What was the outcome?

SITUATION 2

Identify a personal leadership situation where, due to your own efforts, you were not pleased with the outcome you achieved.

(NB: this could be a situation where you were the actual leader, i.e. the manager, or a more temporary leadership role, e.g. a project management role or where, due to particular circumstances, you assumed a leadership role.)

Recall the events and prepare your thoughts and make some notes to share with your coach.

Consider:

- What was the context?
- Who was involved?
- What were the events leading to the situation?
- What happened? Recall what you (and others) thought, said and did
- How did you feel? (Consider both during and after)
- What was the outcome?

At the start of the coaching session I introduce the leadership styles framework using the following diagram. I prefer to use Hay Group's terminology as I feel 'directive' is less emotive than 'coercive' and that 'visionary' and 'participative' are more accurate descriptions than 'authoritative' and 'democratic'. I point out that all of the styles have their time and place and that there are no 'good' or 'bad' styles. The key is to select the appropriate style for the appropriate situation.

I then proceed to talk through the six styles with my coachee, seeking their observations, examples and insights. At the end of each style description I invite my coachee to assess how much they use this style, either using the following leadership style wheel or a simple 1 to 10 rating scale, 10 being 'I use this style all of the time' and 1 being 'I hardly ever use this style'.

The six styles are briefly summarised below. For a more in-depth appreciation I would recommend reading Goleman's *Leadership That Gets Results*.

The Directive Style. This style is characterised by giving directives and expecting immediate compliance. The

Figure 20 My Leadership Styles Wheel

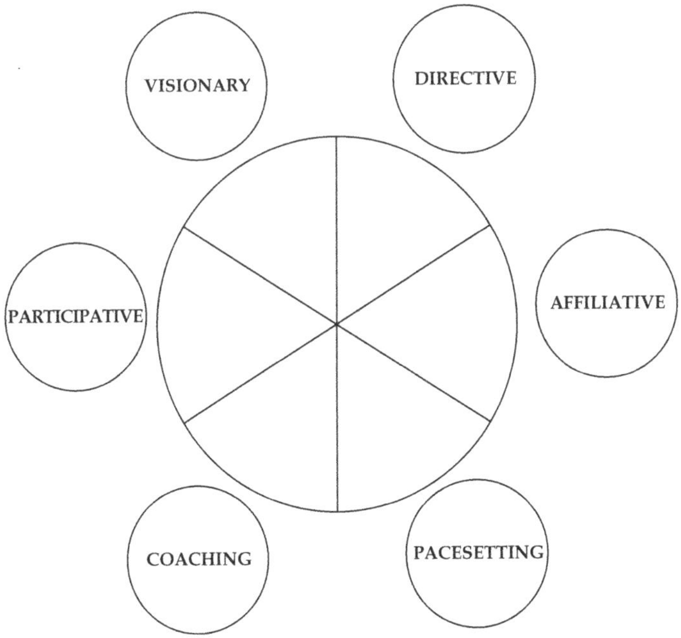

overall tone of the style is 'Do what I tell you'. The leader maintains tight controls and tends to rely on negative corrective feedback. If overused the style has a long-term negative impact on the climate of the organisation. However, it can be useful in the short-term – for example in a crisis, to kick-start a turnaround, when deviations from compliance will result in serious problems and with problem employees.

In my own coaching practice I have come across clients who over-rely on this style and, as a result, do little to grow and develop their staff. I've also had coachees who avoid this style like the plague for fear of confrontation and, as a result, problem employees continue in their existing ways and challenging conversations don't take place. In such circumstances the focus of the coaching may be on preparing for and having that challenging conversation; being more assertive and/or giving that tough feedback.

The Visionary Style. This style seeks to mobilise people towards a vision. The leader focuses their energy on developing, articulating and selling a clear vision, soliciting employees' perspectives on the vision and seeking to get employees on board by selling the 'whys' in terms of the employees' and/or organisation's long-term interest. The overall message is 'Come with me' and the style is effective when changes require a new vision or when a clear direction is needed. Goleman's research concluded that, of all the styles, the visionary style has the most positive impact on the organisation's climate. However, over-reliance on this style may mean that important immediate tasks are overlooked. It is also least effective when the leader does not develop employees or is not perceived as credible.

258

The Affiliative Style. With this style the leader's modus operandi is all around creating harmony and building emotional bonds. The mantra is 'People come first' and, as a result, energy is spent on promoting friendly interactions, addressing employees' personal needs and aiming to keep people happy. This style can be highly effective in the short term, for example to heal rifts in a team or motivate people during stressful circumstances. However, in the long term it can result in too much emphasis on personal needs rather than tasks/standards, with a consequential drop in the latter.

I find 360° feedback a valuable source of information with regard to over or underuse of this style. Highly affiliative leaders tend to attract positive comments such as 'X is a great person' or a 'great team player' with little focus on tangibles. Their team is regarded as a nice and happy place to work rather than a high performing team that consistently delivers to high standards. Equally, the leader who underuses the affiliative style may receive feedback that team members don't feel they know much about them, what their outside interests are, what makes them tick, and their interactions are strongly task based.

The Participative Style. This style seeks to forge consensus through participation. The leader is often heard asking 'What do you think?' as they seek to build buy-in or consensus or to get input from valuable employees. Time is spent encouraging participation and holding meetings to listen to employees' concerns. The style can be effective with competent employees, when there is more of a focus on coordinating employees' efforts rather than managing them, and/or when the leader is unclear about the best approach – for example when managing a multi-disciplinary team. However, the style is less effective in crises or with employees who are not competent, lack crucial information or need close supervision.

The Pacesetting Style. The title says it all. The pacesetting leader leads from the front with the mantra 'Do as I do, now!' Performance standards are high; there is little sympathy for poor or under performance, and the pacesetting leader delegates reluctantly. Equally, responsibility is taken away if high performance is not forthcoming or delegated tasks are not completed quickly. The pacesetting leader loves rescuing a situation and, if they are honest, a good crisis. The style is highly effective when there is a need to get quick results from a highly motivated and competent team and for developing employees who are similar to their leader. However, it is a short-term style and is less effective when it is impossible for the leader to do all of his/her work personally or when employees need direction, development and coordination.

In my coaching and leadership work I meet a lot of pacesetting leaders, especially when working with people who are making the transition from doing the job themselves to looking after a team of people responsible for an overall function. The compulsion to carry on delivering is still there. Typically, pacesetters recognise themselves from this description immediately – in particular the reluctance to delegate. Equally, they recognise the downside of overusing this style – long hours, poor work-life balance and the danger of burnout.

The Coaching Style. The focus of this style is on developing people for the future. Leaders who have a strong coaching focus work with team members on identifying their strengths/weaknesses and encouraging employees to establish long-range goals. The leader can often be heard saying 'Try this', providing ongoing instruction as well as feedback, and may trade off immediate standards of performance for long-term development. In Goleman's research this style comes after the Visionary Style in having the most positive impact on the climate of the organisation. The style can be highly effective with employees who are motivated to seek professional development, but is likely to be less effective when employees require considerable direction and feedback, there is a crisis situation or when employees are not interested in long term professional development.

Having described the six leadership styles and invited my coachee to self-score themselves, I then invite them to comment on their leadership wheel or scores.

What strikes them about their scores/their wheel?
Do they tend to favour long or short term styles?
Which styles do they over/underuse?
What insights do they have from the activity?

Next I invite my coachee to refer to their pre-work and share with me both of their leadership situations – the one they were pleased with and the one they were less pleased with. After they have described each situation I ask them to reflect on which of the leadership styles they believe they used and the effect these styles had on the climate relating to the people involved. Having done this exercise with many of my coachees in the past, I am struck by how consistent the responses tend to be. Typically, in the 'less pleased with' scenario coachees reflect that they only used one or perhaps two styles and often selected the 'wrong' style for the situation. For example, they jumped in and completed the task themselves when it could have been a fantastic coaching opportunity. Equally, in the 'pleased with' scenario, coachees reflect that they actually used a range of styles, maybe all of them, and had been adept at selecting the right style for the right situation. This is consistent with Goleman's initial research findings.

> *The styles, taken individually, appear to have a direct and unique impact on the working atmosphere of a company, division or team, and, in turn, on its financial performance. And perhaps most important, the research indicates that leaders with the best results do not rely on one leadership style; they use most of them in a given week – seamlessly and in different measure – depending on the business situation.* (Goleman, 2000, p.2).

Finally I invite my coachee to consider what is going to be important for them to pay attention to as a leader going forward. By this stage coachees have typically 'got it'; they know what they need to do and are already starting to think of specific action and opportunities to practise using other styles.

AUTHENTIC LEADERSHIP

The other aspect of leadership that frequently seems to find itself on the agenda in coaching is that of authenticity. Coachees often carry around a somewhat idealised view of a leader – someone who is outgoing, charismatic, has presence and gravitas – but are concerned that they are naturally none of the above. Instead their personality is more introverted; perhaps they feel a bit awkward in formal social settings, they don't perceive themselves as having charisma, and they've certainly never been told that they have.

On several occasions, coachees have said to me, 'Leaders are born, not made, aren't they?'

My personal belief is that there are certainly personality traits that make a leadership role a more natural fit for some people. However, that is certainly not the whole story, and if we look at some of the people we admire as leaders, either people we actually know or know through their public persona, we can see that leadership comes in a range of different shapes and sizes.

I frequently find myself recommending Goffee and Jones's book, *Why Should Anyone be Led by You?* (2006) to coachees who are wrestling with this idea of being authentic. The whole book is built on the premise of 'Be yourself… more…with skill', i.e. how we balance authenticity and skill. Goffee and Jones explore four different combinations of skill and authenticity at work as follows:

- Skill and authenticity combine to produce leadership.
- Individuals have a strong sense of who they are, what made them and what they stand for, but they lack the skills to deploy their attributes. They may fail to read contexts, to communicate well, and to see the world through the eyes of potential followers.
- Individuals have considerable interpersonal skills but have a lack of groundedness, which means that followers often feel that they are being worked, manipulated and sometimes exploited. They never display enough humanity to become really effective leaders.

- Low levels of both self-awareness and skill combine, resulting in rather clumsy and unsophisticated skills and behaviour.

Goffee and Jones argue that acquiring skills is rather easier than increasing authenticity. Much standard training and development is concerned with the former; the latter takes longer and requires deeper interventions.

Goffee and Jones go on to explore the characteristics of some of the most talked about leaders and what it is that makes them stand out as leaders, concluding that there are no hard and fast rules, but there are some common themes. The themes are, I believe, controversial and, at times, challengeable, but I believe they do nevertheless form the basis of a good discussion on leadership brand. These themes include:

- **Having personal differences that form the basis of your leadership capability.** What differences have the potential to excite others, are genuinely yours (not copied from someone else) and signify something important in your context? These could include your personal values and vision for those you are leading. In short, what is your unique selling point (USP) or brand as a leader?
- **Revealing personal differences that form the basis of your leadership capabilities.** Goffee and Jones argue that it is a trap to pretend that you are perfect. On the other hand, your leadership is unlikely to be enhanced by the revelation of all your weaknesses, or by fallibilities that vitally undermine your performance. Effective leaders are able to focus others' dissatisfaction around personal foibles

that, paradoxically, make them more human and so more attractive. A case in point would be Nelson Mandela: someone who undoubtedly was a great leader and had an amazing ability to connect and build rapport with people from all walks of life. Yet Mandela would have been the first to say that he was no saint and his personal life and relationships were somewhat chequered.

- **The ability to read different contexts,** including picking up and interpreting soft data. How well are you able to pick up on subtle shifts in the behaviour of others? Are you equally adept with bosses, peers, subordinates, customers, competitors? With those you like as well as those you dislike? How do you adapt across cultures? Are you better one-to-one, in a small group or large gatherings?

- **Do you conform enough?** As a new leader the drive is often about making a mark, getting noticed. However, we are unlikely to survive for long if we cannot recognise the moment to hold back. We are also unlikely to connect with others if we cannot find common ground. This characteristic is about our ability to gain acceptance with others – without losing our authenticity.

- **Managing social distance.** This is about the ability to get close to those we lead. Knowing the goals, values and motives of those who have the biggest impact on our performance. What do we need to know more about? Equally, are we able to separate and create distance from others when we need to? An aspect I find is a particular challenge when coachees find themselves managing people who used to be team members and/or are close friends.

- **Communicating effectively.** This last characteristic can be thought about in various ways. For example, how well we communicate our personal differences, our weaknesses, values and vision. Another important aspect is understanding when we are at our best. Are we better in formal or informal contexts? Are we effective in personalising our communications – perhaps through humour and stories? Can we adapt to the different needs of different followers? Here the focus should be on managing our weaker areas and maximising the areas that we are best at.

The above characteristics are, I find, useful food for thought and never fail to promote a good, robust discussion on what makes a leader as well as promoting some self-reflection on own leadership brand and unique selling point. This is also a great opportunity to encourage your coachee to reflect on his/her strengths and relative areas of weakness. Are these weaknesses serious and likely to become 'derailers' or can they be compensated by further developing strengths? (For a more in-depth look at strengths see Chapter Twelve.) Equally, the Neurological Levels of Change Model (covered in Chapter Eight) is a very useful way of helping someone appreciate just how aligned or congruent they currently are as a leader. How well does what they are doing (behaviour) in their current role sit with their personal values and beliefs? If they are aspiring to be a highly effective leader (identity) how well is this aspiration supported by their current skill levels? Do they need to develop some additional skills? Do they need to let go of some existing behaviours?

I was recently coaching David. David's role had changed and he had moved from being a well-respected technical expert with no direct reports to being in charge of a small team of professionals. David's manager had recommended coaching to help David develop his leadership style and also raise his profile in the organisation. When I met with David he described how he felt he needed to be more like his manager. The company used the Insights Discovery Model and he described how his manager had lots of sunshine yellow energy. By contrast he was predominantly 'Cool blue with a small amount of fiery red'. He went on to explain that he felt he needed more tools and strategies to be 'more yellow' and generally more outgoing and sociable. As he stated this apparent goal he did so with little enthusiasm. It came across as something he felt he ought to be doing.

I asked David what he thought about people who were very sunshine yellow. What impact did they have on him? He immediately volunteered that he tended to find them quite irritating; they spoke too much, and often the topics were of little interest to him and shallow. I then asked how well being more sunshine yellow sat with him. Was it a good fit for him? No was the immediate reply. It wasn't a good fit, and yet he wasn't sure how else he could be. That was the model he had in mind and what he felt his manager expected.

We went on to explore leadership styles. Perhaps unsurprisingly David had a dominant Pacesetting style and was very low on Affiliative, Coaching and Participative. We also explored the idea of Authentic

Leadership, which really resonated with David. He totally understood the idea of being himself…more… with skill and was very open to exploring a more skilful but still authentic David. In particular, David reflected on how he was currently communicating with his team and how this matched his own abilities and preferences. Since assuming his new role he had been arranging meetings with all team members present. This was resulting in rather unwieldy meetings and David was frustrated that no one else seemed to be really bought into the meetings, and he also hated having to lead such big meetings.

'So why continue to have them?' I asked.

We went on to explore the communication channels David was comfortable with and used effectively. He enjoyed one-to-one meetings and so he decided to set up weekly one-to-ones with his direct reports. The wider team meeting became a monthly meeting, and David decided to run this in a more participative way – preparing a detailed agenda in advance and asking team members to lead on specific topics. David's manager had been encouraging him to organise a fun team away day, which he hated the thought of, but he was happy to facilitate an away day focussing on the team's vision and objectives for the coming year, followed by a team dinner. He started having lunch with team members as a way of getting to know team members better and developing his Affiliative style. He even organised a collection and card for a team member who was about to go on maternity leave. The last time I met with him he took great pride in describing the fantasy football league he had put together for the team which all team members were participating in, and for which he'd arranged a prize of a magnum of champagne.

By the time the coaching assignment concluded, David and his manager were pleased with his results. He hadn't become full of sunshine yellow energy overnight. However, he had flexed his style. He had become less Pacesetting and developed his Affiliative, Participative and Coaching styles, and had done so in a way that played to his strengths and was congruent with who he was. He was well on the way to being himself...more... with skill.

In summary, for me, leadership skills coaching is all about working with a coachee and facilitating their learning and development so that they become the best version of themself. The best leader they can be whilst be true to their own personality and working preferences – i.e. their authentic self. My coaching approach therefore starts with my coachee exploring who they are and what makes them tick followed by reflection on how they can develop and enhance their own style.

O chestnut tree, great-rooted blossomer,
Are you the lead, the blossom or the bole?
O body swayed to music, O brightening glance,
How can we know the dancer from the dance?

WB Yeats

CHAPTER FIFTEEN

TIME TO REFLECT

I think it is rather fitting that the final chapter of this book is titled Time to Reflect. Time and time again my coachees tell me that one of the most powerful benefits they have experienced from coaching is having some quality thinking and reflection time. One coachee told me recently that she really valued the couple of hours she spent with me. It slowed her down, gave her time to think, permission to press the pause button and allowed her to put things into perspective. After one coaching session she thanked me and commented on just how useful the session had been – it had really clarified her thinking on a knotty issue and she now knew what she needed to do. I smiled to myself as I had actually asked her very few questions and had given her no ideas of my own. My role had primarily been that of a sounding board, or a mirror where questions and comments were reflected back to her, and this process succeeded in giving her some clarity. Another coachee, new to coaching, told me that he was finding the time to reflect on things invaluable. In addition, he commented, the journey back to his office afterwards was hugely productive as he was spending this time making plans, thinking about how he was going to put his learning into action.

I have heard the whole coaching experience described as 'Like spending time with yourself, having your thoughts reflected back and having a conversation with yourself'. As a coach, when we are actively listening and encouraging what Nancy Kline refers to as 'generative thinking', our role is similar to that of a mirror. Reflection in coaching can, I believe, happen at a number of different levels. There's the reflective space during the coaching itself: an opportunity for the coachee to slow down and reflect on what is happening in a particular situation. There's the reflection after the coaching session and in the gap between that and the next session. There is also the final, and perhaps lengthier, reflection at the end of the coaching assignment focussing on how successful the coaching has been from the coachee's perspective. Finally there are the coach's own reflections on their practice.

We're going to explore each of these forms of reflection in this chapter.

REFLECTING – FROM THE COACHEE'S PERSPECTIVE

I recently asked a number of coachees to complete the following sentence: 'Working with a coach is like…' This question is taken from the Clean Language Compass illustrated in Figure 3 in Chapter Four and its specific purpose is to invite the coachee to answer it in terms of a metaphor or analogy. I asked this question as I was particularly interested in the metaphors and analogies coachees would use and if there was any commonality in these. The most common theme arising out of this question was that, at its best, working with a coach is like having an extension of self.

Tom's account captures the essence of this analogy.

Gill: *Working with a coach is like…?*

Tom: *Talking to yourself, but getting more out of it.*

Gill: *What is the more?*

Tom: *Getting through the frustration piece and coming up with a plan. Talking to yourself and getting out of the mire.*

Pete answered the same question in a very similar way, stating: '...Like having a conversation with yourself. Having a sensible conversation with yourself is probably a more accurate phrase'.

Pete described how he would often go into a coaching session with everything jumbled in his mind and how his coach would ask questions back in a coaching manner and he would walk out of the session clear about what he needed to do. For Pete it was:

> *Jumbled thinking, jumbled mind, feeding it into a computer and that computer helping me to think about it clearly, about the next actions that I needed to take.*

Claire used a different but related metaphor, stating, '... Like taking a long, hard look in the mirror, which you wouldn't normally do', a sense that the coach's questions and presence enabled Claire to take the time to step back and look at herself in a more objective manner.

For Nicola, the analogy went even deeper:

> *It's partly like having a conscience, someone who is your conscience, who tells you what you really know and how you know you should really behave. That old thing – look at the mirror in the morning and be sure you're doing the right thing.*

For Sarah, a high energy individual, reflection appeared to be something that she had not previously made time for, and she highlighted how working with her coach had provided this opportunity:

Sometimes with John it's been about spending time just to have a chat about things I'm doing and how I'm approaching things. Otherwise, when do you stop to do that sort of thing?

Another coachee, Mike, was quite clear about how much he had benefited from reflection and he identified the technique as one of the most powerful ones he had learned:

The value of spending some time reflecting on things. The fact that it's under my own control to manage and change things. We used a lot of reflection. It's a very valuable process of stopping and talking through something. Although I don't have a coach now I'll sometimes go and have a coffee with someone and just have a chat as my way of making space.

So, creating the time and space for our coachees to slow down and reflect is, I believe, one of the key ingredients of sustainable coaching. Indeed, when I'm talking to potential coachees during a chemistry session I take care to stress that time to reflect is one of the key benefits of coaching. I also stress that if the coachee has a natural high energy pacesetting style that they may find the more reflective pace of coaching rather different and perhaps a bit challenging at first.

At the end of a coaching session, once we have agreed actions and 'homework' I always press the pause button and invite my coachee to reflect on the session. Typical questions I ask include:

- *So how did you find the session?*
- *What particularly resonated for you?*
- *What didn't really work for you?*
- *What did I do that worked for you/you found useful?*
- *What could I have done more/less of?*

Equally I always start a coaching session with reflections following the last session. I usually start with the following open question: 'So, what were your reflections on our last session as you were travelling back, soaking in the bath, etc.?'

I find this a useful question as it gives me a sense of how much reflection my coachee did immediately after the session – did they continue exploring an issue in their own mind, did they go off and immediately put something into action or did they simply go to their next meeting.

I will then typically follow up with a question along the lines of: 'So where are you in your thinking and feeling today?'

I consciously make this question quite vague rather than a specific 'How are you?' question.

My intention is to get an insight into how my coachee is right now. I am conscious that my coachee is not in the same space as he/she was when they last saw me a month ago. Time has moved on, events have happened, and I want to create some space for my coachee to reflect on what has happened since we last met and where they are in their thinking and feeling right now as we start the next coaching session.

END OF COACHING REFLECTIONS

The next form of reflection I'm going to cover is the coachee's reflection at the end of the coaching assignment.

I usually work with my coachees over a number of months, during which we have a number of coaching sessions, typically six. At the end of the penultimate session I suggest we spend some time at the next, final, session both reflecting on the overall process of coaching and what the coachee has got from it as well as exploring how they are going to sustain their learning once our regular sessions have ceased. In readiness for this session, I let my coachee know that I will be sending them some questions to aid this reflection. I suggest that they take some time to reflect on the questions and jot down some responses which they can either email to me in advance or bring along on the day. The questions I ask are as follows:

- Thinking back to our coaching sessions, what do you remember? What has stayed with you as useful, challenging or relevant?
- What was the balance of support and challenge in our coaching?
- How has your work benefitted from your participation in coaching? What is different or better in your work?
- How effective have you been in meeting your coaching outcomes/goals?
- Thinking about how we have worked together, what has been most effective for you?
- What specific actions would have improved the quality of our coaching arrangement?
- How will you sustain the learning you have taken from this coaching and apply it in your ongoing work?
- Thinking about how I have worked with you as your coach, is there anything you would like me to have stopped? Started? Increased? Decreased?

Here these questions have two purposes: to encourage the coachee to reflect on their own learning and what has changed, and to provide me with some feedback so I can reflect on my own coaching practice – what went well, what interventions have been particularly useful, what didn't work as well for this coachee, have I slipped into bad/old habits?

THE COACH'S REFLECTIONS

In order to grow and develop truly as a coach we need to be able to reflect upon our practice: what went well, what did not go as well and the potential reasons why, and draw on this learning for future coaching interventions. Schön and Argyris, working in the field of professional education, named this practice 'Reflective Inquiry'. Their view was that skilled professionals who are faced with challenging and often complex worlds need a way to stay open to themselves and to keep checking on the impact of their interventions on clients to ensure their effectiveness.

Schön distinguishes between two types of reflection: reflection in action and reflection on action. The former is that part of ourselves that observes and reflects on what we are doing as we are doing it. Casement coined the term 'the internal supervisor' to capture this type of reflection within the world of psychotherapy. As we engage with our coachees we become our own supervisor: monitoring, thinking, evaluating, assessing what is going on. It's a way of making sense of what is happening as it is happening. This ability to reflect effectively in action comes with experience.

The second form of reflection, reflection on action, is a more luxurious reflection when we stop activities and intentionally put ourselves into a state of reflection. We are provided with time, space, safety and attention to focus on and think about our experiences. Supervision mostly uses this second type of reflection.

COACH SUPERVISION

Supervision has been an essential part of counselling for many years, but has only recently started to become regarded as best practice for coaching. Most of the coaching professional bodies are now advocating regular supervision for coaches, although there are differing views on the regularity of supervision and the experience/qualifications required to be a supervisor.

Carroll and Gilbert (2005) describe supervisors as 'facilitators of learning' and a supervisee as 'one who brings his/her work to another (individual or group) in order to learn how to do that work better'. Supervision is an invitation to look into your work in the presence of another skilled person, the supervisor.

Coach supervision is therefore about coming into a space where a reflection process can take place. This can include aspects of work which feel troublesome or you need help with professionally, relationship issues, process issues and issues of CPD. Jochen Encke in *Passionate Supervision* uses the analogy of supervision as providing the space for 'the box', i.e. the safe place where we store problems, to be broken open and the contents examined. It's a place to explore what is happening, including our tendencies to edit, sensor and make assumptions. Supervision provides an opportunity to perceive experience afresh.

The process of supervision maps nicely on to Kolb's Learning Cycle:

- The coach does their work (Concrete Experience/Feeling)
- The coach stops their work and starts reflecting (Reflective Observation/Watching)

- The coach draws out their learning from their reflection (Abstract Conceptualisation/Thinking)
- The coach then applies their learning to new situations (Active Experimentation/Doing)

As someone who is not a natural reflector, and who really used to struggle with the reflection stage of the learning cycle, I have found regular one-to-one supervision and group supervision an excellent way of helping me develop a more reflective practice. Carroll and Gilbert (2005) describe this process of developing reflective practice through supervision as the distinction between the 'internalised supervisor' and the 'internal supervisor'.

With the former, Carroll and Gilbert argue that during the process of supervision a supervisee moves away from relying on their own internal critic towards utilising the wisdom and experience of a supervisor. In this process the supervisee will take into their own internal mental world their real life supervisor's attitude and ideas. In practical terms this means using the wisdom and suggestions of their supervisor to support their work. This could be very literally following the advice of a supervisor and even using his/her words in working with people – a sense of 'I could hear your voice in my head' or 'I knew exactly what you would say at this point and I found myself saying the same words'. Carroll and Gilbert argue that this marks the internalising of the supervision and a shift in learning from conscious incompetence to conscious competence.

By contrast, Carroll and Gilbert argue that developing your own internal supervisor involves integrating everything that has been learned from your supervisor and everything from your reflections, experimenting, observations, learning and reading. It requires developing your own criteria for good practice and being able to judge whether you are being effective or ineffective in your work. This may involve digesting what you've learned and changing and/or retaining some aspects. Arriving at this stage would similarly involve a shift in learning – this time from conscious competence to unconscious competence.

The amount and level of supervision you require as a coach of course depends on how much coaching you are actually doing – whether it's just a part of your role or a substantial part of your work. As such, supervision can take various forms. Peer supervision can be an effective way of sharing concerns and getting some different perspectives on situations. Peer supervision can either be one-to-one or in groups.

One of the difficulties with peer supervision is the ease with which a supervision session can turn into chat or giving advice rather than helping the supervisee draw out their own learning. In addition, whilst peer supervision can provide a useful support forum for newly qualified coaches, it can also be limiting. For example, what happens when someone raises a concern that no one in the group is sufficiently experienced or qualified to answer? Group supervision where a small group of coaches, ideally up to six, take part in supervision facilitated by a qualified supervisor is therefore an alternative option. Group supervision enables participants to hear about the work of others and issues similar to their own and to get a sense of what peers are struggling with. Equally, my own experience of being part of supervision groups is that others have knowledge and experience that I don't have, and so there's always some rich learning.

However, group supervision may not be for everyone. Much of the success of the experience will be down to the makeup of the group, how much or little participants contribute (dominating or holding back) as well as the logistical issues of getting a group of busy people together. As with coaching, establishing a contract, both for how the group will work together as well as for an individual session, is a useful means of ensuring that the group stays on track. The contract would typically cover logistical issues, for example how often the group will meet, as well as other ground rules – time boundaries for sessions, how the time will be split equitably so that all group members have their turn and what aspects of work will be brought to the group.

Finally, for those wanting to have more one-to-one time there is the option of individual coach supervision sessions.

The main coaching bodies provide details of their requirements for supervision, including how to find a qualified supervisor. A useful contacts list is provided in Appendix One.

REFLECTION FROM SUPERVISION IN ACTION

'So have you got anything that you'd like to bring to the group today, Gill?' my supervisor asked.

I paused. I'd been wrestling with whether to tell my group about my work with one of my coachees, Tony. I'd been working with him for some time now, and after our last session I'd had a sense that we were going backwards, not forwards. I was frustrated and not sure what was going wrong. I decided to go for it.

'Yes, I'd like to share my work with Tony.' I continued that I would like some insights from the group as to what might be going on, and also to think about what I could do differently in our next session as I would be seeing him the following week.

I described to the group how Tony had a specific long-term outcome that he was working on and I had suggested that he identified some baby steps as interim goals. He had duly done so, but his baby steps appeared like great strides to me. It felt as if we were going around in circles.

I paused, and a member of the group asked me, 'If I was standing on the balcony watching the two of you performing a dance, what dance would it be?'

I didn't even pause. 'The trouble is Tony is trying to do a waltz and I'm doing a jive. We're just totally out of synch.' I paused, and nobody broke my silence. I then continued, 'And the sad thing is, I think we have the potential to do a really elegant foxtrot together.'

The group fell silent again, and then another member gently probed.

'I notice you keep referring to baby steps. You are even making step motions with your hand, and I'm wondering if that is your metaphor or Tony's.'

The question stopped me mid stride. I had not even thought of that, yet when I reflected, the metaphor had totally come from me. I had introduced the idea of baby steps and kept referring to them. I wondered if perhaps I was almost talking a foreign language to Tony. Did he have any idea what I was talking about? The session ended with me deciding to share my reflections with Tony at our next coaching session.

The following week I had a coaching session with Tony. I started it off by saying, 'I've been reflecting on our conversation last time. I'm aware that I kept talking about baby steps and encouraged you to identify some. But I've been wondering if that analogy is meaningful for you. Does it even make sense? Is there a better way of looking at your outcome?'

Tony responded immediately. 'No, it absolutely does make sense. The problem is, though, that I have no idea what a baby step is like.'

Finally it clicked. 'Are you up for looking at step sizes?' I asked. Tony nodded. I immediately got a sheet of paper and wrote down 1 to 10. We started talking about some of the baby steps Tony had identified for himself and, as we did so, plotted them against a score. It took some time, but eventually we got there. Not surprisingly, the baby step Tony had identified for himself previously he actually scored at 8. Tony ticked off 3 and 4 – he had done these – and turned his attention to number 5 on the list. We both laughed: we finally had a common language.

The above story is, for me, a great example of the power of reflecting on your practice in supervision. Could I have got to the same point reflecting on my own? Well, maybe, but maybe not... Sometimes I think we can be so close to the issue, so caught up in the dynamics of the situation, that we need help to gain a different perspective. Which is why I would advocate that regular supervision is vital for coaches who are truly seeking to improve their coaching practice.

We shall not cease from exploration
And the end of all our exploring
Will be to arrive where we started
And know the place for the first time.

'Little Gidding', The Four Quartets,
T.S. Eliot

CONCLUSION

My intention in writing *Coaching With Impact* was to create a manual, a practical toolkit, which developing and would-be coaches alike could use in their everyday work and coaching practice. I hope you have found the tools and techniques included useful and that I've inspired you to introduce some of these into your own coaching practice as well as thinking about some creative ideas of your own.

Coaching is a skill, and the only way to develop a skill is through practice. Think back to any of the skills you've developed over the years – be it learning to drive, learning a musical instrument or playing golf. Yes, you may have had some innate talent, but developing high level proficiency requires practice. There are no short cuts. Coaching is the same. To become a highly effective coach requires skill and practice – focused practice incorporating action, reflection and feedback and the application of acquired learning into new action.

So, my challenge to you as we reach the end of this book is to reflect on your development as a coach. You may want to refer back to the Characteristics of an Effective Coach exercise in Chapter One and your current level of proficiency which you captured in Table 1. Where do you need to focus your attention in order to develop your skill as a coach?

The answer to the above question may be quite straightforward, for example my listening skills or my use of clean questions. Equally you may conclude that you are currently a fairly good all round coach, in which case what would it take for you to take your coaching to the next level?

In recent years, the concept of the 'aggregation of marginal gains' has gained popularity when focussing on performance improvement. The phrase was first used by David Brailsford, General Manager and Performance Director of the cycling team, Team Sky. When Brailsford joined Team Sky in 2010 no British cyclist had ever won the Tour de France. Brailsford created a goal to do just that in five years. His strategy for doing so was built upon the belief that if you improved every area related to cycling by just 1% then these small gains would add up to a significant improvement. Initially these marginal gains were quite obvious ones – nutrition programmes for the cyclists, targeted training programmes, the ergonomics of the cycling seat and the weight of the tyres. But Brailsford didn't stop there. He continued to look for 1% improvements in tiny but less obvious areas – investigating which pillows offered the best sleep and taking these to the hotels the cyclists would be sleeping in; selecting the most effective massage gel; and even training the cyclists in the best way to wash their hands to avoid infection.

Brailsford believed if Team Sky could execute this marginal gains strategy successfully then his five year timeframe was realistic. In fact he exceeded his expectations. In 2012 Sir Bradley Wiggins became the first British cyclist to win the Tour de France. That same year Brailsford coached the British team at the London Olympics. The team dominated the competition, winning seven out of ten track medals.

So what are your marginal gains which, if aggregated, would really enhance your performance as a coach?

When thinking about how to conclude this book, I found my mind being drawn to a conversation I had with Oscar several years ago. Oscar had worked with a coach for several months, and I'd asked him if ultimately, in the long run, he thought it had made a difference. I vividly recall how Oscar had reflected for a while and then provided the following eloquent metaphor:

A while back I remember reading about someone who said the best golf lesson he ever had was when he went along to a pro and the pro watched him and said, 'That's really good and just try this little thing instead.' He only ever touched one tiny thing at a time. The pro was always saying, 'That's good, that's good, just try this...' And by the end of his lessons he realised he'd changed every single thing about his swing, but the way the pro had done it was by always saying that what was happening was good, and why didn't he think about something different over here? And that was my experience of coaching. At the end of it – I know I said I wasn't sure how much I'd really changed – but at the end of it we'd touched on so many things that nothing was radically changed, but everything was better tuned. Yeah.

Reflecting on this quote now I think it is also applicable to coaching skills. Those starting out as coaches often tell me that they feel there is so much to learn, so much to pay attention to, that they can feel quite overwhelmed and reluctant to have a go in case they make mistakes. However, taking Oscar's golf coach analogy and focussing on practising one small thing at a time and reflecting on what worked and what could have been better or different before then trying something else is a great way of developing coaching skills.

So now you have come to the end of this book, I'd like to invite you to take a few moments to reflect on your insights and learning from the book. What has resonated with you? What has been useful? What has challenged your thinking? What have you learned and how are you going to apply that learning? Take a moment to capture your reflections. And now pick one small thing, have a go, take action…

USEFUL WEBSITES

Author's website *http://www.iridiumconsulting.co.uk*

Association for Coaching *http://www.associationforcoaching.com*

Capp *http://www.cappeu.com*

Career Anchors *http://www.careeranchorsonline.com*

Chartered Institute of Personnel and Development *http://www.cipd.co.uk*

Coaching Supervision Academy (CSA) *http://coachingsupervisionacademy.com*

European Mentoring and Coaching Council *http://www.emccouncil.org*

Institute of Leadership and Management *http://www.i-l-m.com*

International Coach Federation UK *http://www.coachfederation.org.uk*

International Coach Federation US *http://www.coachfederation.org*

OH Cards Institute *http://www.OH-Cards-Institute.org*

Rory's Story Cubes (*http://storycubes.com*)

BIBLIOGRAPHY
AND REFERENCES

Argyris, C. and Schön, D. (1978) *Organisational learning: A theory of action perspective*. Reading, Mass: Addison Wesley

Berne, E. (1964) *Games People Play*. London: Penguin

Blakey, J. and Day, I. (2012) *Challenging Coaching, Going beyond traditional coaching to face the FACTS*. London: Nicholas Brealey.

Bluckert, P. (2005) 'The foundations of a psychological approach to executive coaching', *Industrial and Commercial Training*, 37, 4, p.171-178.

Buckingham, M. & Clifton, D.O. (2001) *Now, Discover your Strengths: How to develop your talents and those of the people you manage*. London: Simon & Schuster.

Carroll, M. and Gilbert, M. (2005) *On Being a Supervisee: Creating Learning Partnerships*. London: Vukani Publishing.

Casement, P. (1985) *On Learning from the Patient*. London: Tavistock.

Clutterbuck, D. (2003) *Managing the Work-Life Balance*. London: CIPD.

Corey, G. (2001) *Theory and Practice of Counselling and Psychotherapy*. London: Brookes/Cole.

Corporate Leadership Council (2002) *Performance Management Survey*. Washington, DC: Author.

Downey, M. (1999) *Effective Coaching*. London: Orion.

Encke, J. (2008) 'Breaking the Box: Supervision – A Challenge to Free Ourselves', *Passionate Supervision*. London: Jessica Kingsley Publishers, Ed. Shohet, R.

Flaherty, J. (1999) *Coaching: evoking excellence in others*. Oxford: Butterworth-Heinemann.

Gallwey, T. (1986) *The Inner Game of Tennis* Pan.

Goffee, R. and Jones, G. (2006) *Why Should Anyone be Led by You?* Boston: Harvard Business School Press.

Goleman, D. Boyatzis, R. and Mckee, A. (2002) *The New Leaders*. London: Little Brown.

Goleman, D. (1995) *Emotional Intelligence*. New York: Bantam Books.

Goleman, D. (May 2000) *Leadership that Gets Results*. Harvard Business Review.

Goleman, D. (Nov 1998) *What Makes a Leader?* Harvard Business Review.

Graves, G. (2010) *Presenting Yourself With Impact*. England: Book Shaker.

Hawkins, P. and Smith, N. (2006) *Coaching, Mentoring and Organizational Consultancy*. Open University Press.

Honey, P. and Mumford, A. (1992) *The manual of learning styles.* Maidenhead, UK: Peter Honey.

Kline, N. (1999) *Time to Think, Listening to Ignite the Human Mind*, London: Cassell Illustrated.

Kouzes, J.M. and Posner, B.Z. (2002) *The Leadership Challenge*. San Francisco: John Wiley and Sons Inc.

Kotter, J.P. (1996) *Leading Change*. Harvard Business Review Press.

Kolb, D. (1984) *Experiential Learning*. Englewood Cliffs: NJ. Prentice Hall.

Laborde, G.Z. (2003) *Influencing with Integrity*. Wales: Crown House Publishing Ltd.

Lawley, J. and Tompkins, P. (2002) *Metaphors in Mind*. London: The Developing Company Press.

Linely, A. and Harrington, S. (2006) *Playing to your Strengths*. The Psychologist, 19, 2.

Parsloe, E. and Wray, M. (2000) *Coaching and Mentoring*. London: Kogan Page.

Rogers, C. (1961) *On Becoming a Person*. Boston: Houghton Mifflin.

Rose Charvet, S. (1997) *Words that Change Minds*. Iowa: Kendall/Hunt.

Rogers, J. (2004) *Coaching Skills*. Buckingham: Open University Press.

Schön, D. (1983) *The Reflective Practitioner*. New York: Basic Books.

Seligman, M.E.P. and Csikszentmihalyi, M. (2000) 'Positive psychology: An introduction', *American Psychologist*, 55, 5-14.

Shatté, A. and Reivich, K. (2002) *The Resilience Factor*. Broadway Books.

Thach, L. C. (2002) 'The impact of executive coaching and 360 feedback on leadership effectiveness', *Leadership and Organisational Development Journal*, 23, 294-306.

Wasylyshyn, K.M. (2003) 'Executive coaching: An outcome study', *Consulting Psychology Journal*, 55, 94-106.

Whitmore, J. (2002) *Coaching for Performance: Growing People, Performance and Purpose*. London: Nicholas Brealey.

Zenger, J.H. and Folkman, J. (2009) *The Extraordinary Leader: Turning Good Managers into Great Leaders*. USA: The McGraw-Hill Companies.

Other resources are available from
http://www.iridiumconsulting.co.uk/books-and-resources/

You may also like to sign up now for Gill's monthly hints and tips newsletter at
http://www.iridiumconsulting.co.uk/books-and-resources/

THE AUTHOR

Gill Graves MA, MBA, FCIPD, is an experienced and highly regarded executive coach, coach supervisor, facilitator and consultant in leadership and team development. She specialises in enabling individuals and organisations achieve their goals and realise their full potential.

Gill is recognised by the European Mentoring and Coaching Council (EMCC) as one of the few Master Practitioners in the UK. She has an MA in Coaching and Mentoring and is an accredited mediator in alternative dispute resolution. Gill is also a qualified supervisor of coaches. Gill has an MBA from Warwick University and is a Fellow of the CIPD. She is a regular speaker at meetings and conferences and is the author of *Presenting Yourself With Impact*.

Prior to founding her own company, Iridium, in 2000, Gill was HRD Director of a US high tech company; she has extensive hands-on international experience, gained within fast-growing, rapidly changing environments. Gill has built an impressive and loyal client base at Iridium, spanning both the public and private sectors in the UK and internationally. Gill's clients include Vodafone, The Open University, Computacenter, IKEA, Suffolk County Council, Faccenda Group, the NHS and Judge Business School.

Gill is happy for you to email her at info@iridiumconsulting.co.uk or contact her via the web at www.iridiumconsulting.co.uk